yourself

small business
accounting

"...a must for every new sole
proprietor"
The Independent

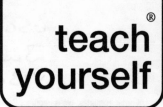

small business
accounting
mike truman

For UK order enquiries: please contact Bookpoint Ltd, 130 Milton Park, Abingdon, Oxon OX14 4SB. Telephone: +44 (0) 1235 827720. Fax: +44 (0) 1235 400454. Lines are open 09.00–18.00, Monday to Saturday, with a 24-hour message answering service. Details about our titles and how to order are available at www.teachyourself.co.uk

For USA order enquiries: please contact McGraw-Hill Customer Services, PO Box 545, Blacklick, OH 43004-0545, USA. Telephone: 1-800-722-4726. Fax: 1-614-755-5645.

For Canada order enquiries: please contact McGraw-Hill Ryerson Ltd, 300 Water St, Whitby, Ontario L1N 9B6, Canada. Telephone: 905 430 5000. Fax: 905 430 5020.

Long renowned as the authoritative source for self-guided learning – with more than 40 million copies sold worldwide – the **teach yourself** series includes over 300 titles in the fields of languages, crafts, hobbies, business, computing and education.

British Library Cataloguing in Publication Data: a catalogue record for this title is available from the British Library.

Library of Congress Catalog Card Number: on file.

First published in UK 1997 by Hodder Arnold, 338 Euston Road, London, NW1 3BH.

First published in US 1997 by Contemporary Books, a Division of the McGraw-Hill Companies, 1 Prudential Plaza, 130 East Randolph Street, Chicago, IL 60601 USA.

This edition published 2003.

The **teach yourself** name is a registered trade mark of Hodder Headline Ltd.

Copyright © 1997, 2003 Mike Truman

Typeset by Transet Limited, Coventry, England.
Printed in Great Britain for Hodder Arnold, a division of Hodder Headline, 338 Euston Road, London NW1 3BH, by Cox & Wyman Ltd, Reading, Berkshire.

Hodder Headline's policy is to use papers that are natural, renewable and recyclable products and made from wood grown in sustainable forests. The logging and manufacturing processes are expected to conform to the environmental regulations of the country of origin.

Impression number   10 9 8 7 6 5 4
Year   2010 2009 2008 2007 2006 2005 2004

contents

introduction

Who is this book aimed at?

This book is intended for the small business owner with no knowledge of – or real interest in – book-keeping and accountancy. It can be used by the smallest of businesses – part-time as well as full-time – and by those who have no aptitude for figures. Provided you can more or less understand what your bank statement means, you can understand this record-keeping system. It does not assume that you know anything at all about business records and accounts; it does not use jargon but it uses practical examples of real businesses (a builder, a village shop and a taxi driver) to show you, step by step, how to record each transaction. It does not just deal with the book-keeping records, but it also tells you how to file records, fill in cheque stubs etc. This is a system for real businesses to be operated by real business people who want a simple, easy and – above all – quick system of book-keeping.

The system outlined is not suitable for a business which needs to keep sales and purchase records on credit for a large number of customers or suppliers. As a rule of thumb, if you can't fit all your sales invoices for the year into one large lever-arch file, and all the purchase invoices for the year into another, you may find this system does not give you enough information. But if the sales are paid for immediately, you *can* use it – it is fine for a corner shop, for example.

The system can cope with straightforward loan financing arrangements, although it does so in an unorthodox way, in order to avoid getting into accounting jargon. It cannot cope easily with a business that runs more then one bank account, although your accountant – if you have one – will be able to explain how to run separate books for each account and how to account for transactions moving between them.

This book is intended mainly for **sole proprietors,** that is people who own their business outright and in person. It is *not* suitable for use by limited companies, even when the only shareholder is also the only director. It is suitable for use by husband-and-wife type partnerships, where there is no need to split the drawings between the two partners. Such partnerships should treat all references to 'the proprietor' as references to either or both partners. The information in Chapter 23 on completing the tax return will be found to apply just as well to the partnership tax return which they will have to complete. More complicated partnerships will probably need further professional advice on the adaptations needed to this system for their purposes.

The record-keeping system explained here is one that you write up by hand, often referred to as a **manual** system. The system can also be computerised very easily by using a **spreadsheet** program. This will eliminate some of the donkey-work involved in using a calculator to add up columns of figures and trying to find mistakes. A few tips on how to set up a spreadsheet are included in Chapter 28, but you will need to be familiar with the basic operation of spreadsheets already in order to use them.

If you use a proper accounting package on your computer, the details of how the transactions are entered will, of course, be different from the system outlined here. However, the information about filing and cross-checking from your invoices will still apply, as will the use of the information in completing your tax return. If the computer package you use is one which is based on the bank account, such as **Quicken**™ or **Microsoft Money**™, then you will find many similarities between the way it operates and the system set out in this book; they actually handle the information in much the same way, it is just that the mechanics of the analysis are hidden from view by the computer. Using this book in conjunction with the manual supplied with the accounting package can therefore often help you work out how to enter unusual transactions.

Why this book is different

If you have looked at other books on accountancy and book-keeping before buying this one, you will know that they are often full of jargon. They talk about ledgers and journals and 'double-entry' – you may feel that you need a dictionary by your side to read them. Do you really *need* to know all this to handle the finances of a small business? No, of course you don't. Most of these books are not aimed at owners of small businesses at all: they are aimed at students taking exams in book-keeping and accounts. Even those that claim to be aimed at business people still try to teach them a version of book-keeping best suited to large businesses.

The system commonly described is called 'double-entry book-keeping'. It has been around for over five centuries, and has stood the test of time. It can be used to produce accounts for anything from a small business to an international company, and it includes a system of cross-checking to minimise the chance of errors. But it is also complicated to learn, and unless you understand it thoroughly it is very easy to enter transactions incorrectly. Moreover, as the name suggests, it involves writing up every transaction twice – once as a **debit** entry and once as a **credit** entry. Frankly, unless you are at the stage where you can afford to have a part-time book-keeper come in one afternoon a week to write up your records, there is no point in running a double-entry system.

Most accountants, when advising small business clients, do not suggest that they keep double-entry books. Instead, they suggest a system similar to the one set out in this book. It is based on your bank statement, with a bit of extra analysis into the categories of income and expense. Unfortunately, accountants do not always have time to explain the system in great detail to their clients. Whilst, in general, it is easy to see how transactions should be entered, there are some which are not so intuitive, and if the business owner does not really understand how to deal with them, mistakes will be made. The detailed explanations in this book will ensure that you can produce a complete and correct set of books for your business.

At the end of the year, you have a choice. If you are using an accountant to deal with your tax affairs, you can present him or her with a complete set of records, fully totalled and cross-referenced. This should save you money, because you do not have to pay your accountant to total columns of figures for you, or search through piles of invoices trying to tie them in to the bank statement. If you are going to adopt this approach, you will only need to read up to Chapter 20, although reading the remaining chapters will probably help you to understand far better what your accountant can do for you.

Alternatively, you can deal with your own tax affairs. The records produced under this system are designed so that they produce exactly the figures you need for the new type of tax return now being used by the Inland Revenue under the self-assessment system. Chapters 21–23 explain, step by step, how to get from your end of year totals to the figures on the tax return. Because the calculation of taxable business profits is more straightforward now, it is much more realistic for a small business owner to consider doing without an accountant.

Of course accountants can handle other financial problems for you, and if you are going to do without one, you need to know how to deal with these problems yourself.

For most small businesses, it is not necessary to produce a 'proper' set of accounts, with a balance sheet. However, your bank manager may want to see one, so Chapters 24–25 explain how you can use these records to produce one. If you want to get an overdraft from your bank manager you will need to provide a **cash-flow forecast**, predicting how much cash will be going in and coming out of your business in the next year or two. Chapter 26 explains how to do that.

Finally, you need to know how to price the goods and services that you offer. Surprisingly, research shows that owner-managed businesses do not normally fail because they overprice. Instead, they often try to compete *only* on price, and as a result pitch their prices too low. This leads to the common experience in running a small business of being rushed off your feet with work, yet still being in trouble with the bank manager because you are up to your overdraft limit.

The key to pricing is to understand your costs; the basic techniques that accountants are taught about costing are explained for you in Chapter 27.

The best way to use this book is first to read it through to Chapter 17. This covers all the basic entries that every business needs to make in its records. Then read Chapters 18 and 19 if they apply to your business, and Chapter 28 if you are thinking of using a computer. If you need information about cash-flow and pricing immediately (for example, because you are preparing a business plan) read Chapters 26 and 27. The time to read Chapters 20 to 25 is probably a few months after you have started keeping records under this system, so that you have a clearer idea of what is involved – you are then better able to decide whether you will need professional help with your end of year accounts and tax return.

Summary

You can use this book if you are:

- a sole trader or small partnership
- with only one bank account
- without too many sales and purchases on credit.

Everyone should read up to and including Chapter 17. Read the other chapters if and when you need them.

case studies

It is always far easier to understand something if you see it being applied. This is particularly important when looking at business record-keeping, because the system has to be explained in general terms, which apply to any business, whereas you need to apply it to your particular business.

Although most books teaching a book-keeping system use examples they are frequently unconnected, so you get no picture of how the use of the system builds up. Additionally, there is often an artificiality about them. For example, most examples tend to be from industry, often dealing with manufacturing, whereas most small businesses are actually in the retail or service sector.

So that you can see the system in operation for different businesses, three different case studies are used in this book. Hardip Singh is a builder, Grace Morris runs a village shop, and Ben Martin is a self-employed taxi driver. Some more background information for the case studies is given below.

Not all the case studies are used to illustrate each chapter. Sometimes one is chosen to illustrate particular problems or unusual transactions that arise in that sort of business and which need to be recorded in a particular way; at other times one business is followed through several chapters so that you can become familiar with the transactions that are being recorded and can better understand what is happening.

When you are reading through the book, try to follow the examples fully. It can be tempting to skip over the detailed figures and get on again to the explanations. The way to get the best out of the book is to follow the examples line by line and fully understand them before you move on.

Hardip Singh – builder

Hardip Singh is a builder. He occasionally works as a sub-contractor for other builders, but normally he works directly for clients, carrying out small building jobs.

He has no permanent staff, but employs casual labourers from time to time. Just because they are casual, this does not mean he can pay them 'cash in hand'. He accounts for PAYE on their wages.

He works from home, where he keeps his pick-up truck and tools, and where he writes up his business records. His wife acts as a part-time secretary for him, taking messages and making some phone calls.

He generally works **on invoice**; that is to say that he gives his customers a bill which they pay later, but sometimes he is paid immediately, either in cash or by cheque. He has an account with a local builders' merchant where he buys most of his supplies, but sometimes he goes to the local DIY store and pays by cheque or credit card.

Grace Morris – shopkeeper

Grace Morris runs a village shop, selling food, sweets and newspapers. The shop is rented, and she and her husband live upstairs.

Her customers pay her as they purchase goods, by cash or cheque. The only exception is newspaper deliveries, for which people come into the shop and pay once every couple of weeks.

Her purchases come partly from the Cash and Carry, partly from wholesalers on invoice, and the newspapers and magazines come from a wholesale newsagent.

She has three paper boys to deliver the newspapers, and some part-time help in the shop.

Ben Martin – taxi driver

Ben Martin is a taxi driver. He works partly by taking people who hail him on the street, and partly through bookings by a company, Cab-U-Like, which provides him with a radio. He is paid almost invariably in cash by the people he picks up from the street. When he takes a Cab-U-Like client he is not paid directly, but receives a cheque from Cab-U-Like at the beginning of each month for the fares he carried in the previous month. His expenses are mainly paid on credit card for fuel etc., in cash for minor expenses and by cheque for the main cab expenses such as servicing etc. He works from home.

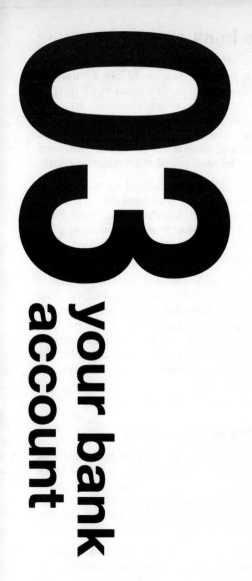

03

your bank account

In this chapter you will learn:
- why you need a bank account
- how to check your recording system
- how to read your bank statements.

Why you need a bank account

If you had a very small part-time business, you probably would not need a business bank account. You could use a modified version of the simple cashbook system, described in Chapter 4, to record all of your income and expenses. However, once the number of transactions goes above about a dozen a month in total (both purchases and sales combined) you need a more formal system of recording and analysis. In particular, you need a way of checking that you have recorded everything correctly.

By using a bank account solely for your business – separate from your normal personal bank account if you have one – you will be able to check your accounting records against your bank statement on a regular basis. This is one of the two main ways this system ensures that you have not made any mistakes. (The other is explained in Chapter 5.)

Another reason for having a business bank account is that it provides some independent evidence of your income and expenditure for the Inland Revenue. They are naturally suspicious of businesses that are conducted wholly in cash, and the evidence of a cheque paid out through your bank account for an amount that matches the invoice in your records for the goods you bought will *always* be more convincing than the evidence of the invoice alone.

Business or private account?

Having said that you need a separate account for your business, that does not necessarily mean that you need to tell your bank to open a business account. Many people trade quite happily using a personal bank account for their business. Unfortunately, for different reasons, they all find that they cannot operate through a personal account so have to open business accounts.

The main reason for this is that it is so much cheaper. Competition between banks and building societies means that at present in the UK it is customary for personal accounts to be free of charges provided they are in credit. When you consider the amount of work involved in processing cheques, issuing statements, collecting money for cheques paid in etc., it is immediately obvious that the banks lose money on the operation of these accounts. For personal customers, because of the competition, they have to accept this and try to recoup their losses by selling other products to their customers such as loans, insurance and pensions. However, business customers normally have to pay the going rate for operating their current account, even if it is always in credit.

Most banks will offer a new business customer **free in-credit banking** for the first year, but, after that, charges can seem very high. You will typically be charged between 50p and £1 for each cheque you write, and the same amount for each payment into your account. Electronic transactions such as direct debits and standing orders may be cheaper; paying in cash can be even more expensive.

This is why many small businesses are run through private bank accounts. Provided the number of transactions does not become excessively large for a private account, many banks will turn a blind eye to this. One way to minimise the number of cheques paid out is to use a credit card to pay for as many expenses as possible, and then pay it off in full each month with a single cheque. Keeping the number of cheques paid in to a minimum is more difficult, and if you pay in a lot of cash on a regular basis you will probably be asked to convert to a business account.

Apart from the number of transactions, there are two other reasons why you may find you have to ask for a business account to be set up. The first is if you trade under another name. Banks will only take cheques made payable to the name of the account holder for a personal account. The other reason is if you need an overdraft – banks will always ask why you want borrowing facilities, and will not normally give you an overdraft to finance a business on a personal account.

Case studies

So how do the three businesses in our case studies organise their banking?

Grace Morris would not be able to pay a cheque made out to 'Village Stores' into her personal account. In any case she needs to be able to pay in cash. She has therefore found a former building society which offers free in-credit business banking, including paying in cash locally. The account is in the name of 'Mrs G Morris t/a Village Stores'. The abbreviation 't/a' means 'trading as' and this means that she can pay cheques into her account made out to either 'G Morris' or to 'Village Stores'.

Hardip Singh trades under his own name, but he often needs an overdraft while he pays for materials and labour that can only be billed when the work is complete. He had little choice but to open a business account with a bank. However, he did not go to the bank where he banks personally. He asked around other builders, and found that several of them banked with an Irish bank that had a branch in the local High Street. It was felt that their staff understood the problems of builders. Always ask people in the same business and the same area as you for their recommendation, and be prepared to go to a bank which is not one of the 'big four'. Be aware, however, that really small banks can be more of a risk.

Ben Martin cannot use a personal account because of the amount of cash he banks. However, if he worked mainly for account customers, so that most of his receipts came as a single monthly cheque from Cab-U-Like, he would probably have been all right. As it is, he also has to use a business bank account from a high street bank.

If you have to use a business bank account because you are using a trading name, but you do not have many transactions going through it and do not need an overdraft, there are some business accounts which offer free-in-credit banking provided you keep below a certain number of transactions each month. Many of these accounts are operated by post or over the internet, and competition seems to be increasing their number.

Bank statements and how to read them

Personal bank accounts generally provide monthly statements. For business accounts you need to tell the bank how often you want statements, since otherwise they may only come quarterly. You certainly need statements at least monthly, and for a business with a lot of transactions it can be useful to have them weekly.

It is possible to get cheque books and paying-in books in different formats, which are suitable for different types of business. *Always* use your paying-in book to make deposits; do not fill in a loose slip at the bank. It is too easy to lose the counterfoils, which form an important part of your records.

A bank statement for a business account is no different from that for a personal account, but you will need to understand exactly what is meant by the various entries. Figure 3.1 below shows a typical bank statement, with various entries highlighted.

A There are two important numbers that you need to know for your bank account. The first is the **account number**, which uniquely identifies your account within the branch. The second is the **sort code**, a six digit number in the form xx – xx – xx, which uniquely identifies your bank branch. These two numbers together identify your bank account from any other in the country. The sort code will not always be on the statement, but will always be in the upper right-hand corner of your cheques. The account number will always be on the statement.

B There will be five columns on the statement. From the left, they show the *date* a transaction was recorded by the bank, the *details* of the transaction, *payments out* of the account (sometimes called **debits**), *receipts into* the account (sometimes called **credits**), and the *balance* after each day's transactions.

• ANYBANK PLC •

STATEMENT OF ACCOUNT

Mr A. N. Other
1 Avenue Road
ANYTOWN
AA1 1ZZ

Account number 765 432 10   Sort Code 12 - 34 - 56 **(A)**

Date	Details	Payments	Receipts	Balance **(B)**
200X				
1 Sept	Balance b/f			256.09
5 Sept	Cheque 300321 **(C)**	100.00		156.09
6 Sept	Cash/cheques **(D)**		326.00	482.09
10 Sept	D/D Friary BS **(E)**	495.00		–12.91 **(G)**
13 Sept	Bank credit **(F)**		643.93	631.02
20 Sept	Bank charges **(H)**	32.00		599.02
23 Sept	Cheque 300224	154.00		445.02
30 Sept	Balance c/f **(I)**			445.02

---

figure 3.1 a typical bank statement

C Cheque payments rarely show anything except the cheque number. For this reason it is very important that you fill in your cheque stub accurately to show what the money was paid for. This is dealt with in more detail in Chapter 7.

D Receipts can sometimes be even less informative. Some banks number the paying-in slips in the book they provide for you; others do not. If they do not, the only information you have to go on is the amount paid in and the date of the transaction. Again, this means that it is vital to record the right information on the paying-in counterfoil. This is dealt with in Chapter 14.

E Standing orders and direct debits can be shown in different ways, usually by an abbreviation such as 'DD' or 'SO', or by using a phrase such as 'By order of'. Whilst you will get more information about the payee, you may not immediately recognise a payment if it is infrequent – an annual subscription, for example. It is a good idea to check your direct debits and standing orders regularly, ensure that you know what they are for and consider whether the product or service concerned is still needed.

F More and more businesses are making payments through automatic clearing systems, which do not require cheques. Typically you will receive a form from a customer saying that in future they would like to make all payments direct to your bank account, and asking for the sort code and account number. When you next send them an invoice, they will not send you a cheque, but will inform you that the payment has been made by a bank transfer. This means that the money has gone automatically from their account and into yours.

G The daily balance will indicate whether you have money at the bank or whether you are overdrawn. Sometimes this is done by putting a minus sign or the letters 'OD' when you are overdrawn and just the figure when you have a positive balance; alternatively the letters 'CR' show that you have a credit balance and 'DR' that you have a debit (overdrawn) balance.

H The bank may have imposed charges or interest for overdrafts or bounced cheques, which will be shown in the payments column. Banks have a poor record on the calculation of overdraft interest. The most common problem is when a new overdraft limit is agreed but is not recorded on the account. Interest is then charged at a penal rate of around 30% as if it were an **unauthorised** overdraft, rather than the rate agreed. You should always check, very roughly, that the charge is reasonable by estimating your average overdraft for the period covered by the interest charge (typically three months), multiplying by the percentage interest rate, and dividing by four for a quarterly charge or twelve for a monthly one.

For example, Hardip Singh has agreed with his bank manager that he can have an overdraft of up to £10,000 at an interest rate of 10%. For the past quarter (i.e. three-month period) he has been charged £130 in interest. Looking at his statements, he has been overdrawn for most of the quarter, on average by about £5,000. Now £5,000 at 10% is £500, divided by four is £125. This is quite close to the figure he has been charged, so he does not query it or check further. Had he been charged, say, £250, he would have tried to calculate the correct figure more accurately and/or taken it up with his bank manager.

I   The statement will start with a **balance brought forward** and end with one **carried forward**. You should remember that this does not take into account cheques paid out that have not yet been cleared, nor deposits made that have not yet been processed.

So now that you understand your bank statement, it is time to look at how to use it to produce business records.

Summary

You need a separate bank account for the business, but it doesn't have to be what the bank calls a 'business account'.

Some banks will offer permanent free banking for businesses, subject to a limit on the number of cheques drawn and paid in.

Know what the entries on your bank statement mean!

Make a rough check of your overdraft interest each quarter.

04

a simple cashbook

The last chapter explained how to read a bank statement and understand what all the entries mean. This chapter shows you how to enter them into a very simple accounting book, called a cashbook. Confusingly, a cashbook does not normally show what has happened to the cash in your business – it shows what has happened to money you have paid into or taken out of the bank. If you want to think of it as a bank book then you can, but it is referred to here as a cashbook because that is what it will be called by an accountant or a tax inspector.

A simple cashbook, as set out in this chapter, would be all that you would need for a very small business – one with fewer than a dozen transactions a month going through the bank. Most businesses will need a slightly more complicated form of cashbook, which is explained in the following chapters. However, that builds on the concepts introduced here, so it is important that you start by fully understanding how a simple cashbook operates.

Essentially a cashbook is a detailed bank statement. It includes all the information that you normally put on cheque stubs, deposit counterfoils and so on to help you identify exactly what you have spent your money on.

Hardip Singh's simple cashbook

In Chapter 2 you met Hardip Singh, a builder. Figure 4.1 shows his bank statement for the month of June.

The following further information is recorded on his cheque book stubs etc:

- Cheque 1000234 was to High St Garage for diesel for his van.
- Cheque 1000235 was to the Anytown Courier for a classified advertisement.
- Cheque 1000236 was to V G Browns for stationery.
- Cheque 1000237 was to Smarts Builders Merchants for supplies, of which £30 was for use in his own home.
- Cheque 1000238 was to Jones Plumbing for supplies.
- Cheque 100239 was to Post Office Counters for road tax on the van.
- Cheque 1000241 was to Print Pronto for business cards and letterheads.
- The payment to County Leasing is the monthly instalment on the lease contract for the van, and the payment to Magnificent Mutual is for his personal pension.

		Debit	Credit	Balance
1 June	Balance b/f			2150.25
3 June	s/o County Leasing	345.22		1805.03
8 June	Ch 1000234	28.34		1776.69
10 June	Dep 6000132		396.75	2173.44
10 June	Ch 1000236	25.68		2147.76
12 June	s/o H. Singh	500.00		1647.76
14 June	Charges	42.30		1605.46
18 June	Ch 1000235	43.69		1561.77
18 June	Ch 1000237	692.59		869.18
20 June	Dep 6000133		2750.00	3619.18
21 June	DD NICO	28.40		3590.78
23 June	Ch 1000238	254.00		3336.78
23 June	Ch 1000239	150.00		3186.78
28 June	Ch 1000241	82.38		3104.40
30 June	DD Mag. Mutual	100.00		3004.40
30 June	Balance c/f			3004.40

figure 4.1 Hardip Singh's bank statement

- The payment to the NICO is for his Class 2 National Insurance Contributions.
- The payment to H Singh is his monthly drawings paid into his personal bank account.

Mr Singh issues an invoice from a pre-numbered **duplicate book** for each job done.

- Deposit number 6000132 was a cheque from Mr Henderson paying invoice 121.
- Deposit 6000133 was a cheque for £2,000 from Mr Peters paying invoice number 118, a cheque for £600 from Mr Bull paying invoice number 119 and £150 in cash from Mr Blunt paying invoice number 123.

Mr Singh only writes his cashbook up at the end of each month when he receives his bank statement. He uses a two-column

PAYMENTS

3 June	s/o County Leasing	(Motor)		345.22
8 June	234 High St Garage	(Motor)		28.34
10 June	236 V G Browns	(Administration)		25.68
12 June	s/o H. Singh	(Drawings)		500.00
14 June	Charges	(Finance charges)		42.30
18 June	Anytown Courier	(Advertising)		43.69
18 June	237 Smarts	(Cost of Sales)	662.59	
	237 Smarts	(Drawings)	30.00	692.59
21 June	DD NICO	(Drawings)		28.40
23 June	238 Jones Plumbing	(Cost of Sales)		254.00
23 June	239 Post Office Counters	(Motor)		150.00
28 June	241 Print Pronto	(Administration)		82.38
30 June	DD Magnificent Mutual	(Drawings)		100.00
30 June	Total			2292.60

figure 4.2 Hardip Singh's payments

cashbook, so that he can enter subtotals, and puts receipts on the left-hand page and payments on the right. Figure 4.2 is his Payments page for June.

Notes

1 Each entry shows the cheque number, the person to whom the payment was made, and the type of expense (in brackets) after it. Some of these will be obvious; for example road tax and petrol are classed as 'Motor'. Some will not be so obvious, such as 'Cost of sales'. The reason for using these specific headings rather than ones that may be more appropriate to your business is that they are the ones you will have to use when you fill in your tax return. If you use them from the start, it makes filling in your tax return much easier. The payments to be included in each category are set out in the next chapter.

2 Any money taken out of the business for your personal use is called 'Drawings'. That includes pension payments, and paying tax and national insurance, so the monthly payment to the NICO is classified as drawings.

3 Provided your cheques run in a numerical sequence from one cheque book to the next, you probably only need to note the last three numbers.

4 The payment to Smarts included £30 for materials Mr Singh was going to use personally, which must be recorded as drawings. So two entries are made for the same cheque, with subtotals in the first column that add up to the total amount of the cheque which is entered in the second column.

5 All the payments are inclusive of any VAT charged.

Mr Singh's Receipts page for June is shown in Figure 4.3:

	RECEIPTS		
1 June	Brought forward		2150.25
10 June	132 Henderson (Invoice 121)		396.75
20 June	133 Peters (Invoice 118)	2000.00	
	133 Bull (Invoice 119)	600.00	
	133 Blunt (invoice 123)	150.00	2750.00
30 June	TOTAL		5297.00
	Less Payments		2292.60
			3004.40

figure 4.3 Hardip Singh's receipts

Notes

1 Because Mr Singh only writes up his records when he has the latest bank statement, the balance brought forward of £2150.25 will be the same in his cashbook and on the bank statement. It is included on the 'Receipts' side of the page because he is in credit at the bank – in total over the previous months and years there have been £2120.25 more receipts than payments. If he was overdrawn at the bank the balance would be brought forward on the 'Payments side'.

2 After the entries have been totalled as before, the total from the payments page of £2292.60 is deducted, to give the balance carried forward of £3004.40.

3 In this case the payments on each separate invoice are listed and totalled. Although this is the clearest way of entering the information, it is not always possible if there are a lot of small receipts. You will learn the different ways that receipts can be scheduled in Chapter 15, and there is an example showing daily takings later in this chapter.

4 The fact that some of the payments are in cash and some by cheque does not matter, since they are all being paid into the bank. Even if cash is not all paid into the bank a way has to be found of entering it in the cashbook, as will be explained in the next example.

Ben Martin's cashbook

Ben Martin writes up his cashbook every week, even though he only gets bank statements monthly. He has a list of his standing orders, and he uses this plus his cheque-book stubs and paying-in records to write up the book. As a taxi driver, most of his takings are in cash, which he banks each weekday after taking out £30 a day as drawings. During the first week of May he wrote three cheques: one to pay off the chargecard with which he buys his fuel, one to pay for hire of the cab, and one to pay for an advertisement in *Yellow Pages*. He also knows that a monthly payment to the Cabdrivers Benevolent Fund has been paid by standing order. Figure 4.4 shows his Payments page for the week:

PAYMENTS			
1 May	Cabdrivers Benevolent	(Drawings)	10.00
3 May	334 Freeway Chargecard	(Cost of sales)	143.80
3 May	335 Taxicab Leasing	(Motor)	350.00
6 May	336 Yellow Pages	(Advertising)	140.00
7 May	Cash contra	(Drawings)	150.00
	TOTAL		793.80

figure 4.4 Ben Martin's payments

Notes

1 The dates are the dates that he wrote the cheques or the date the standing orders are due to go out. They will not necessarily be cashed in this order – it depends how quickly the recipients bank them. This means that the balance on Mr Martin's cashbook will not necessarily tie up with the balance on the bank statement. The process of checking which cheques and deposits have not yet cleared through the bank account is known as **bank reconciliation** and is described in detail in Chapter 17, although most readers will be familiar with it from dealing with their personal bank accounts.

2 There may be other payments which have gone through the bank account – charges, for example – which Mr Martin will only find out about when he gets his statement. They will be entered in the cashbook as part of the bank reconciliation.

3 The reason that Mr Martin's fuel costs are categorised as 'Cost of sales' rather than 'Motor' is that this is what the Inland Revenue insist on for taxi-drivers and others in the transport industry. One of the reasons is that they would expect fuel to be a similar proportion of takings for all taxi-drivers, since the further they drive the more money they should be making.

4 The item 'Cash contra' clearly refers to the £30 a day drawings from the takings, but it is not obvious why this needs to be entered in the cashbook. In order to understand this, it is important to look at Mr Martin's Receipts page in his cashbook as shown in Figure 4.5:

	RECEIPTS		
1 May	Balance b/f		2496.92
3 May	Takings banked	116.67	
	plus cash contra	30.00	146.67
4 May	Takings banked	68.56	
	plus cash contra	30.00	98.56
5 May	Takings banked	94.63	
	plus cash contra	30.00	124.63
6 May	Takings banked	72.49	
	plus cash contra	30.00	102.49
7 May	Takings banked	80.60	
	plus cash contra	30.00	110.60
	TOTAL		3079.87
	Less payments		793.80
	Balanced c/f		2286.07

figure 4.5 Ben Martin's receipts

Notes

1 It would be completely impractical to enter each separate fare that Mr Martin has received, so instead it is simply the day's takings that are entered.

2 The total takings on 7 May, for example, are £110.60. However, only £80.60 was banked. If the only figure entered into the cashbook was the £80.60, the takings (and eventually Mr Martin's profit) would be understated by £30. The best way to avoid this is to pay everything into the bank and then take out the cash by cheque, but that would incur extra bank charges.

So the next best approach is to *imagine* that all the takings had been banked and the drawings taken by cheque. **Contra** entries are used to do this – the word *contra* means that there are corresponding entries on both the receipts and payments side of the cashbook which cancel each other out. On the 'Receipts' page the cash drawings are added back to the takings to arrive at the true amount Mr Martin received from passengers and, as we have already seen, on the 'Payments' page the £30 a day is shown as a payment out. These can be entered daily or, for convenience if the amount is regular, as a weekly total. To illustrate both approaches, a daily entry has been shown on the 'Receipts' page and a weekly total on the 'Payments' page; in practice it is better to be consistent on both sides of the cashbook so that the corresponding entries can be easily identified.

When to update the cashbook

As we have seen, there are two different ways of updating the cashbook. It can either be prepared from the bank statement after it is received, or it can be done as you go along, and then reconciled to the bank statement when it comes in. Neither way is right or wrong – different approaches will suit different businesses.

The advantage of updating the cashbook only when the bank statement is received is that it is easier at a later date to compare the two. The final balance on the cashbook should always agree with the final balance on the statement, so it is easier to find mistakes. Also it generally takes less time overall to sit down for a few hours each month with all the necessary records to update the cashbook rather than spend an hour or so each week, or fifteen minutes each day.

The advantage of keeping the cashbook up to date as you go along is that you always know what the true balance at the bank would be, if all cheques were cashed and all deposits credited. Even if (as is more normal) the cashbook is not totalled in ink at the end of each week, it is common to keep a daily or weekly running total in pencil in the margin.

Also, because it will take a few hours, it is easy to put off the job of updating the cashbook each month, whereas a daily or weekly routine may be easier to keep to. In general, the more important it is for you to have a clear idea of how much money is at – or owed to – the bank, the better it will be to update the cashbook as you go along.

Cashbook analysis

Looking back at Mr Singh's cashbook, it is easy to see how a statement of income and expenditure could be prepared from it. His total receipts are the £5297.00 total on the Receipts page of the cashbook less the £2150.25 that he started with – £3146.75. All of the items on the Payments page can be gathered together under their expense categories as shown in Figure 4.6.

Motor	(345.22 + 28.34 + 150)	£	523.56
Administration	(25.68 + 82.38)	£	108.06
Drawings	(500 + 30 + 28.40 + 100)	£	658.40
Finance charges		£	42.30
Advertising		£	43.69
Cost of Sales	(662.59 + 254)	£	916.59

figure 4.6 Hardip Singh – expenses

However, even with the very limited number of transactions going through Mr Singh's accounts, it is still easy to miss one when calculating these totals. As soon as the number of transactions increases to say 20 or 30 a month, a lot of extra work will be required.

In order to simplify the process of calculating totals for each category and each month, the cashbook can be expanded so that the amount is recorded first as a total and then in a separate column for each expense or receipt category. This is known as an **analysed cashbook** and is at the heart of the accounting system explained in this book. The format of the analysed cashbook is explained in the next chapter.

05

analysis columns

In this chapter you will learn:
- how to create analysis columns
- the different expense categories.

Layout

Figure 5.1 shows how the payments side of Hardip Singh's simple cashbook, which you saw in the last chapter, would look in an analysed cashbook. If you are not very comfortable with figures, this may look rather daunting. Spend some time comparing it with Figure 4.2 in the last chapter, and you will see that there is nothing to be worried about.

The first two columns of the analysed cashbook are almost exactly the same as the first two columns of the simple cashbook, showing the date and the details of the payments from the bank statement. The only difference is that the category of expenditure (motor, drawings etc.) is not now recorded in brackets as part of the details. The third column of the analysed cashbook is exactly the same as the last column of the simple cashbook – it just shows the amounts paid out of the bank account.

However, there are now more columns to the right of the 'Total' column, each headed with one of the categories of expenditure which was recorded as part of the details of the payment in the simple cashbook. There were six categories used, so there are six additional columns for the analysis.

Looking at the first entry, £345.22 paid to County Leasing for leasing the van, this was categorised in the simple cashbook as 'Motor'. So in the analysed cashbook, as well as 345.22 being entered in the 'Total' column, it is also entered in the 'Motor' column.

The next payment is cheque number 234 to High Street Garage. This is also a motoring expense, so £28.34 is entered in the 'Total' column and in the 'Motor' column.

The next payment is to V G Browns for stationery, categorised in the simple cashbook as 'Adminstration'. In the analysed cashbook, the amount paid out of £25.68 is entered in both the 'Total' column and in the 'Administration' column.

All the other entries are made in a similar way, but you should look particularly at the entry for 18 June, cheque number 237 to Smarts. The total of £692.59 was made up of £30 for goods used privately, categorised as 'Drawings' and the balance of £662.59 for materials used on a job, categorised as 'Cost of sales'. In the simple cashbook these had to be entered as subtotals and totalled up. In the analysed cashbook, £692.59 is

Date	Details	Total	Motor	Admin.	Drawings	Finance	Advertising	Cost of sales
3 Jun	s/o County Leasing	345.22	345.22					
8 Jun	234 High St Garage	28.34	28.34					
10 Jun	V G Browns	25.68		25.68				
12 Jun	s/o H Singh	500.00			500.00			
14 Jun	Charges	42.30				42.30		
18 Jun	235 Anytown Courier	43.69					43.69	
18 Jun	237 Smarts	692.59			30.00			662.59
21 Jun	DD NICO	28.40			28.40			
23 Jun	238 Jones Plumb.	254.00						254.00
23 Jun	239 Post Office	150.00	150.00					
28 Jun	241 Print Pronto	82.38		82.38				
30 Jun	d/d Magnificent Mutual	100.00			100.00			
30 Jun	TOTALS	2,292.60	523.56	108.06	658.40	42.30	43.69	916.59

figure 5.1 Hardip Singh – analysed payments for June

entered in the 'Total' column, £30.00 in 'Drawings' and £662.59 in 'Cost of sales'.

This illustrates an important rule about analysed cashbooks. **For every entry, the total of the amounts entered in the analysis columns must be the same as the amount entered in the total column.** Provided a business is not VAT-registered, most entries will only have one amount in an analysis column, which matches the amount in the 'Total' column; but if, as in the Smarts entry, there is more than one amount they *must* add up to the amount in the 'Total' column.

Looking at the totals, you can now see that it is far easier to total up the expenditure for each category. That is the main reason for using analysis columns. For example, when using the simple cashbook there were four different entries categorised as 'Drawings' scattered over the page. Making sure that you didn't miss any in calculating the totals in Figure 4.6 could be difficult, and if there had been – say – fifty entries instead of twelve, it would have been impossible. Now you simply have to add up the figures in each column in order to arrive at a total of expenditure in the month for each category. If you compare the payments summary in Figure 4.6 with the totals for each column in Figure 5.1, you will see that they match.

The other important point to note is that **the totals of the analysis columns should be the same as the total of the 'Total' column.** In other words, looking at Figure 5.1, if you add up 523.56 + 108.06 + 658.40 + 42.30 + 43.69 + 916.59 you will get a total of 2,292.60.

This system of using analysis columns is the most important thing in this book that you have to understand. Spend some time with it to be sure that you completely grasp it. Make up some figures of your own, or use your personal bank statement to analyse your household expenses into different categories – food, clothes, rent or mortgage etc. – using this analysis system. If you can master this concept, it will all be easy from now on. Whilst there are some transactions that are slightly more complicated (see Chapter 8) and you have to learn how to apply the same principle to receipts (see Chapters 15 and 16) they are all based on the same simple concept.

Expense categories

As was explained in Chapter 4, the suggested columns for analysis in this book are based on the categories used by the

Inland Revenue in the self-assessment tax return. These are listed below, with details of what should be included under each heading. Whilst much of this is self-evident some items are surprising and you will probably have to return to this chapter quite frequently, to decide exactly which heading covers a particular expense. You should also get a copy of the 'Notes on Self Employment' from the Inland Revenue, which gives a more detailed explanation of the expenses covered by each heading, and looks in more depth at the expenses which are not claimable against tax. If you are already in business you should have received a copy with your last tax return, but if you are just starting you probably will not have received one – write to your local Tax Enquiry Centre, which will be listed in the telephone directory, and ask for a copy.

The tax return and its guide assumes that you will enter all business expenditure in the accounts, and then separately identify expenses which are not allowable for tax purposes. This seems a pointless exercise, and it is suggested that you should aim to classify most disallowable expenses as drawings. The general rule is that you cannot claim an expense unless it is wholly and exclusively for business purposes. It must also be a **revenue item**, not a **capital outlay**. The question of which expenses are allowable is dealt with in more detail in Chapter 9, and the purchase of equipment is dealt with in Chapter 10.

Cost of sales are the supplies or raw materials that you either consume or resell, if you are in a manufacturing or sales business. Taxi drivers, minicab drivers and haulage businesses should include their fuel expenditure here; everybody else should use the category of motor expenses. No other service business is likely to use this column, although there may be an entry in the tax return after an end of year adjustment.

Subcontractors is apparently only to be used by those in the construction industry for payments to subcontractors. Payments in other businesses, such as payments to a locum, are to be included under employee costs.

Other direct costs – the concept of direct and indirect costs is not one that you are likely to have to understand, and there are very few expenses that fall into this category. Include hire of machinery (other than motor vehicles) and rechargeable expenses: i.e. an expense that you have to pay initially, but which you then recover from your client. If you are not sure whether an expense belongs here or in another category, it is probably the latter.

Employee costs are not just salaries for employees, but payments to subcontractors other than construction industry subcontractors, recruitment agencies, benefits for staff etc. Do *not* include your own wages: these count as drawings. It may, however, be worthwhile paying a salary to your spouse if he or she has no other job, but you will have to be able to show the Inland Revenue that the work performed is genuinely worth the payment made. See Chapter 19 for more details about wages.

Premises costs include rent, heat, light, insurance etc. For the typical small business operating from the owner's home, an adjustment at the end of the year for use of own home may be all that is needed. This is covered in Chapter 23.

Repairs cover both those to business premises and to machinery etc. Improvements cannot be claimed; so for example adding a garage to the home in order to store business materials is an improvement and not claimable, whereas repairing the roof of the existing garage where business materials are already stored is claimable.

General administrative expenses is a catch-all heading for office expenses such as telephone, stationery, postage, business subscriptions etc. This is where a lot of expenses for most businesses are going to end up.

Motor expenses should be self-explanatory. Car repairs go here, not under repairs.

Travel and subsistence include any travel other than motor expenses, plus the cost of hotel accommodation etc. while on business trips. You can only claim for meals if away over night.

Advertising includes direct mail, promotions etc. Entertainment of customers, suppliers, contacts etc. is not allowable. Entertainment of staff is an allowable expense, but may mean that the staff are liable to tax on a benefit in kind.

Legal and professional fees include payments to lawyers, accountants and architects, for example. You cannot, however, claim fees or fines for breaking the law, nor fees which relate to the purchase of fixed assets such as machinery or property.

Interest should be self-explanatory.

Other finance charges include bank charges etc.

Other business expenses – there shouldn't be much that falls in this category; most general expenses will come under the administration heading.

You also need two further columns:

Drawings – in which you include everything that is a private expense rather than a business one, including items such as entertaining customers which you may feel is a business expense but is not in the eyes of the Inland Revenue.

Purchase of equipment – as already mentioned, this is dealt with in detail in Chapter 10, but you need a heading under which to record the payments.

Summary

- A simple cashbook is no more than a bank statement with some extra explanation.
- An analysed cashbook separates the different types of expense out into different columns.
- By entering each figure twice, once in the total column and once analysed across the expense columns, it is possible to cross-check the entries.
- By splitting the expenses according to the Inland Revenue's categories, and only entering allowable expenses, the completion of the tax return is simplified.

06 payments – filing

In this chapter you will learn:

- how to file invoices
- how to manage your creditors
- how to deal with suppliers' statements.

This chapter and Chapters 7 and 8 take you step by step through the process for recording your payments. This chapter looks at filing, the next at what to record in your cheque book, and Chapter 8 looks again at the entries in the cashbook, concentrating on some of the more difficult transactions. These chapters do not deal with payments made by credit card or by cash; those are dealt with in Chapters 11 and 12 respectively.

From now on you will find references in the chapters to the different items of business stationery that you will need; these are summarised on page 179 in Appendix 1, as a shopping list. However, you should read the book first, so that you understand exactly what you need and how it is to be used.

Filing invoices

To file your invoices, you need a large A4 lever-arch file, and a matching hole punch so that you can punch filing holes into any invoice that does not already have them. You also need a divider card, either one that you get in a pack from a stationer's or just a sturdy piece of cardboard that is slightly larger than A4. Finally you need a stapler and a pad of A4 paper.

The system is simple and straightforward, with three basic rules:

1 The invoices are filed in the order that you pay them.
2 Each invoice has the date of payment and the number of the cheque sent in payment written onto it.
3 Invoices are kept on top of the dividing card while they are unpaid, and underneath it when they are paid.

Example

It is 31 March. Grace Morris has just been to the Cash & Carry to buy some stock costing £865. She paid by cheque, number 456. On the way back she puts petrol into her estate car, paying £20 by cheque number 457. When she gets back to the shop she opens the post to find a bill dated 28 March from one of her suppliers, Universe Chocolates, for £245, payable within 28 days. She files this on top of the divider card in the lever arch file. As she does so, she looks through the other invoices still on top of the divider card, and finds that she has an invoice from Browns Wholesale, who supply her with newspapers and magazines, which is overdue for payment. She pays this, £156, with cheque number 458.

You can see illustrations of the invoices in Figure 6.1 below. Follow carefully now what she does with them – the illustrations already indicate what she writes on them.

figure 6.1 Grace Morris' invoices

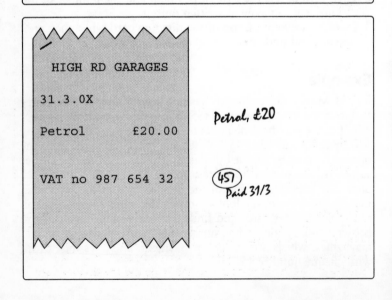

O & Q Cash and Carry
Suppliers to the trade

3 Invicta Way, Camtown CC1 2BB

Mrs Grace Morris
Village Stores
Camtown
CC11ZZ

INVOICE	31.3.0X
Standard-rated Goods	456.00
Zero-rated Goods	320.20
VAT@ 17.5% on standard-rated goods	79.80
	856.00

Paid by cheque

VAT no 123 654 00   (456) Paid 31/3

```
HIGH RD GARAGES

31.3.0X

Petrol      £20.00

VAT no 987 654 32
```

Petrol, £20

(457) Paid 31/3

Browns Wholesale

Newspapers and magazines

The Business Park, Camtown CC1 9AA

Mrs Grace Morris
Village Stores
Camtown
CC11ZZ

INVOICE   29.2.0X

Goods supplied   **156.00**

ZERO-RATED FOR VAT

VAT no 123 654 78
Payable strictly net 28 days

UNIVERSE CHOCOLATES

A taste of heaven

1 Industrial Way, Slough, SL1 1AA

Mrs Grace Morris
Village Stores
Camtown
CC11ZZ

INVOICE   28.3.0X

Goods supplied   **254.00**

Price includes VAT

VAT no 123 456 78

Payable strictly net 28 days

The invoices need to be filed in the order in which they were paid from the cheque book. The first cheque she wrote was number 456, for £865 to the cash and carry. She writes '456' on the invoice and circles it so that it can easily be seen, and 'Paid 31/3'. She then files the invoice immediately below the divider card.

The next cheque she wrote was number 457, for £20 of petrol. Because she only has a till roll receipt for the petrol, she staples it to a sheet of A4 paper, then writes 'Petrol, £20' onto the A4 sheet, because the ink on till roll receipts is prone to fading. She then writes '457' and 'Paid 31/3' on the sheet, and files it on top of the cash and carry invoice, below the divider card.

The last cheque she wrote was 458, for £156. Again, she writes '458' and 'Paid 31/3' on the invoice, tears off the remittance slip to be sent back with the cheque, then files it on top of the petrol invoice, underneath the divider card. Even though this invoice probably dates from some time in February, it goes on top of the other invoices because they are filed in the order they were paid, not the order they are dated. She sends off the cheque together with the tear-off remittance slip from the invoice. The invoice from Universe Chocolates stays on top of the divider card awaiting payment.

Managing your creditors

The people to whom you owe money for goods or services supplied on invoice are your **creditors**. Managing your creditors is an important part of business economics, and can make the difference between a business surviving or failing.

Because this system clearly separates the paid from the unpaid invoices, for a small business it is rarely necessary to have a formal system for reviewing unpaid invoices – just check them quickly every time you open the file. If you don't have very many invoices, so the file can be left unopened for weeks at a time, you may have to have some sort of reminder system, or make a habit of checking it at the end of every week.

Whilst it will improve your credit rating with suppliers to pay them on time, it is pointless to pay them ahead of their normal terms. If you are offered 28 days to pay, take more or less that length of time – do not pay as soon as you get the invoice. It is better for you to keep your bank manager happy by having the money in your account.

If you do find that it is getting difficult to pay your creditors on time, do not fall into the trap of paying the 'squeaky wheel' – the one who shouts loudest. Try to keep paying off the oldest invoices first, although you may have to make an exception for major suppliers who refuse to send further supplies until they are paid, and for rent on your business premises, since you should avoid breaching the terms of your lease. But in general, if you have a good record of paying on time in the past, most suppliers will let you go a few weeks over the due date for payment without causing any great trouble.

If you do not pay your creditors by the due date, then they have the legal right to charge interest at a prescribed rate, and also to charge a fee for the administrative work of chasing the invoice. At the time of writing, these statutory provisions had only recently been brought fully into force and are only used for very late payments, but if they become more commonly enforced then businesses may have to adjust their payment patterns.

Statements

Suppliers may send you monthly statements, showing outstanding invoices. Be careful not to file these as if they were invoices, otherwise you may end up paying the same bill twice. The best way to use a statement is as a reminder that you have an invoice that needs to be paid, and to check that the invoices shown as unpaid on the statement are still filed as unpaid (i.e. on top of the divider card) in your lever-arch file. Provided you are happy with what the statement says, you can normally just throw it away.

Ideally, you should not pay using the remittance slip on the statement, particularly if the statement covers two or more invoices, because it will be difficult to match up the single payment to the different amounts on the invoices. If you do have to do this (for example, because you have a lot of invoices from the same supplier which you want to pay with one cheque) staple the invoices to the back of the statement and write the cheque number on the front of the statement, then file them all together underneath the divider card.

Everything said above about statements also applies to reminders, such as a 'red' telephone bill. Even if you send back the red remittance slip with the payment, make your notes about payment on the original bill and file that, throwing the red reminder away, or stapling it to the back of the original bill. You may want to tear off the original remittance slip and throw that away as well, just to make it clear when you look at the file that the bill has been paid.

No invoices

Not every payment will have an invoice, but if it is a business payment it should have some matching documentation in the lever-arch file. If it is a personal payment, which is clearly marked on the cheque stub as drawings, then this is not so important, but it is a legal requirement that you keep records which are sufficient to identify your business expenses.

Example

Hardip Singh pays a neighbour £25 by cheque, for the use of her garage to store some hired machinery for a few weeks. The neighbour did not give him any form of signed receipt. Mr Singh makes a note on an A4 sheet of paper 'Paid to Mrs Robertson for use of garage next door to store machinery, £25' and writes on it the cheque number and the date of payment in the usual way. This is filed in his lever-arch file in the same place as an invoice would have been filed. It would be far better if he could get Mrs Robertson to sign the sheet as having received the money, but at least he now has a record and a sufficiently clear explanation of why this is being treated as a business payment.

Summary

The result of this filing system is a steadily growing file of invoices or other notes of expenses underneath the dividing card, all in cheque number order, and therefore also in the order in which they were paid. There may not be an invoice or record for every cheque, but if there is not it should be because the payment is a personal one, which will be recorded as drawings in the cashbook. If the payment is a business expense but there is no invoice, then there is a sheet of paper in the right place in the lever-arch file giving details of what the payment was made for.

Even before you read the next two chapters, it should be clear to you that this system means you can very easily find the supporting paperwork for any cheque payment, explaining exactly why the payment was made.

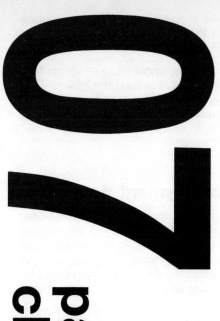

07

payments – cheque book

In this chapter you will learn:
- the importance of payment details
- what to record in your cheque book.

In the last chapter there were several references to writing cheques, but none to the way that the cheque book stub should be completed. That is the subject of this chapter.

The aim of the system for recording payments is to ensure that the essential information is recorded in *at least* two places. That way, if you do lose an old set of cheque book stubs, or a file of invoices, or even your cashbook for a year, it would be possible to reconstruct what was in it from the other information that you have.

The importance of payment details

The most important thing that you need to note on the cheque book stub is the purpose of the payment. The main aim of your book-keeping system is to identify business income and expenses and record them under the appropriate categories for submission to the Inland Revenue. So if you pay your car tax by cheque, the most important thing to write on the cheque stub is 'Car tax'.

The next most important piece of information is whom the cheque was paid to. In the case of your car tax, that would normally be 'Post Office Counters Ltd.'. Now, perhaps, you can see why this is not as important as recording the purpose of the payment; if your cheque stub only told you that you had made a payment to the post office you might think it was for stamps.

The third most important thing to note on the cheque stub is the date that the invoice you are paying was issued. This lets you check in either your cheque book or your invoice file if someone rings you and wants to know whether you have paid a particular invoice.

The fourth most important thing is the date that you are actually writing out the cheque, since the only other place that this is recorded is in your invoice file. If you are postdating a cheque (writing a date on it that is later than the current date) record both dates on the cheque stub.

Perhaps surprisingly, the least important thing to note on the cheque stub is the amount the cheque was made out for. That's not to say you shouldn't bother, just that if you forget you will be able to find the amount on the invoice and confirm that you made the cheque out for the right amount when your bank statement comes. In practice most people remember to write in the amount; it is the payee, the relevant dates and the purpose which they forget. It is far more difficult, and time-consuming, to try to get these details right later – it only takes a few seconds to complete them at the time you write the cheque.

Example

Look again at the first example in Chapter 6, dealing with Grace Morris. Figure 7.1 below shows the cheque book stubs as she filled them out. Remember that she wrote two cheques for goods she had just received. Because these were not on credit there is no need to write in the dates of the invoices, since this is the same as the date of payment.

31.3 200X	31.3 200X	31.3 200X
Stock O & Q	Petrol, High St Garage	Papers, Browns Inv. 28.2
£865.00	£20.00	£156.00
1--456	100457	100458

figure 7.1 Grace Morris' cheque stubs

Example

Turn back now to Figure 4.4 on page 21, showing Ben Martin's payments for the first week of May. He wrote three cheques: one paying off the chargecard for his petrol, one for hire of the cab, and one for an advertisement in *Yellow Pages*. Figure 7.2 below shows how he would fill in his cheque stubs.

3.5 200X	3.5 200X	3.5 200X
Petrol	Taxi lease	Advert
'Freeway' Inv. 14/4	Taxicabs Leasing Inv. 18/4	Yellow Pages Inv. 30/3
£143.80	£350.00	£140.00

figure 7.2 Ben Martin's cheque stubs

Missing details

You may have read through the explanation above and felt that it was a detailed explanation of something that should be very obvious. In practice, when accountants are preparing the books and accounts of small businesses they frequently find that the details on some cheque book stubs are either completely missing or are incomplete. Remember that a brief note that makes perfect sense to you when you write it may not mean anything when you are asked to explain it by an tax inspector or VAT officer a year later. So get into the habit of filling in your cheque stubs correctly, You may even want to write the following five points down inside the cover of your cheque book, so that you remember to complete them all.

1 Purpose
2 Payee
3 Invoice date
4 Date written
5 Amount

If, for any reason, you do not use a cheque (for example, if you make a mistake in writing it out) put a line through the cheque stub and write 'Unused' on it. Try not to do this too often; it will arouse the suspicions of any tax inspector or VAT officer who looks at your accounts, and he or she will check carefully that the cheque with this number did not clear through your bank account.

Running totals

You may be used to keeping a running total in your personal cheque book, subtracting the latest payment from the previous balance, adjusting for any deposits and standing orders that you know about, and writing the new balance on the back of the cheque stub. You can do this if you want to on your business account, but unless it is a very small business you will probably find that it is difficult and time-consuming. You probably write more cheques on the business account, and you will almost certainly have more frequent payments into the account. It is generally better to keep track of the balance in your account either by having more frequent statements sent to you, or by writing up the cashbook as you go, keeping a running total in pencil. This is explained in Chapter 15, after you have learned how to enter receipts in the cashbook.

Old cheque books

When you finish a cheque book, you need to keep the cheque book stubs safe and you also need to be able to find the right book quickly when you need it. The easiest way to lose an old set of cheque book stubs is simply to leave it loose in a desk drawer. At the very minimum, you should keep all your old books of stubs together, in order, fastened by an elastic band. However, a better approach is to start a file that will eventually hold all your records for the year.

Buy a box file, and write the tax year on the outside. Because the tax year ends on 5 April, it is convenient to keep 31 March as your year end, since it is the nearest month end to the tax year. For various technical reasons, this will also keep the complexities involved in calculating your tax bill to a minimum. It is assumed in this book that your year end is 31 March; if you want to use any other year end you should ask your accountant or the Inland Revenue to discuss with you the consequences of doing so, since the details are beyond the scope of this book.

So your file might say 'Year ended 31 March 2003'. Write on the outside cover of the book the range of cheque numbers that it covers; for example '231 – 280'. Keep this in the box file, together with any other cheque books that were finished during the year, fastened together in order with an elastic band. The file will seem very empty at present, but you can also use it to store things such as guarantees for goods bought during the year and correspondence that explains any of your transactions. You should also store your used books of paying-in slips here.

It is at the end of the year that this box file comes into its own. Eventually it will contain a file of your paid invoices for the year, issued invoices for work done in the year, the bank statements for the year and a copy of your tax return: in short, all the records that you need to keep in case of an Inland Revenue or VAT inspection.

08

payments – cashbook

In this chapter you will learn:
- more about analysis columns
- how to complete the 'payments' side of the cashbook.

This chapter builds on the explanation in Chapter 5 about analysis columns, and shows you exactly how to complete the 'Payments' side of the cashbook. The layout of the example given in Chapter 5 was slightly simplified so that you could understand the basic principle of analysis; where there are differences between the layout in Chapter 5 and in this chapter, you should follow the example given here.

Buying a cashbook

The sort of book that you need is sold in stationery shops. Typically they are around A3 size, that is to say the size of two standard sheets of A4 paper side by side. When opened up, a double page looks something like Figure 8.1. There is space at the top for an overall heading and then headings for each of the columns. The three columns on the left of the spread are different from the others. The first column is designed to record the date, the second column is a wider column for written details, where you will put the name of the person to whom the cheque is paid, and the third column is a narrow one, sometimes referred to as a **folio** column where you will put the cheque number.

After that there are several columns for recording cash amounts. You should buy a book with 32 cash columns (that is to say 32 columns in addition to the three already mentioned).

Heading up the cashbook

Inside the front cover of the book print your name, address and telephone number clearly. Even if you intend to deal with your own affairs, it may be necessary at some time for the book to be taken away for examination by the Inland Revenue or Customs & Excise, and if it is separated from the rest of your records it may be difficult to find out who it belongs to.

It is best to start the book at the beginning of a business year. To make your tax liability easier to calculate, you should start your business year on 1 April unless that is a particularly difficult time because of seasonal fluctuations in your business. If you are now reading this book some months later, but still want to use this book-keeping system straight away, it will be far more useful if you go back to the previous 1 April and write out all the records from then, using this system. Although it will take some time, you will save more time at the end of the year. If you are already

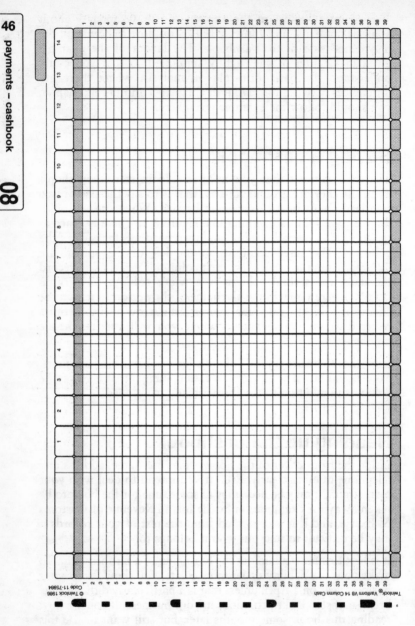

figure 8.1 The double page of a cashbook

in business and use a different year end you can continue to do so, but you will have to bear in mind that the dates given in this book are based on a year that starts on 1 April.

Figure 8.2 shows how the top of the page looks after you have written in the headings, although the difference in size between this book and your cashbook means that only a few of the analysis columns are shown.

At the top of the page, write in the name of the bank, the sort code and the account number. Apart from being an easy place to find these details when you want them, it prevents problems in matching up the cashbook to the bank statements if you should change banks. You also write in the month and the year – you will start a new page at the end of every month.

The entries for payments will take up all of the left-hand page and part of the right-hand one. Head the column on the extreme left 'Date'. The next column (the wider one) should be headed 'Payments out'. The small column next to it is headed 'Cheque no.'.

The next column, which is the first cash column, is headed 'Total'. Leave the following column blank: you will use it later when checking off the payments to the bank statement, and to adjust for any brought-forward overdraft. Head the columns after that with the categories listed in Chapter 5 – only miss one out if you are sure you will have no expense of that type. List them in the same order as they are given in Chapter 5. This should be the order that you will find them on the tax return. This will probably take you to about the sixteenth cash column. You can read about how to set out the rest in Chapter 15, dealing with receipts. If you are VAT registered, you will also need to add a column for that, as explained in Chapter 18.

Writing up the cashbook

To start the cashbook, you need to enter the current balance at the bank, adjusting if necessary for any cheques written or deposits made before 1 April but not reflected in the bank statement at that date. You will only have to make this adjustment if you are going to write up the books from your records as you go along – if you are going to write them up when you receive the bank statement you start with the opening balance on the statement.

The reason for entering this balance is so that you can easily check at any time what your bank balance is, by adding up all the figures in the 'Total payments in' column and in the 'Total

Bank account no 123 456 78   Sort code 12 34 56   April 200X

Date	Payments out	Cheque number	Total	Cost of sales	Subcontract.	Other direct costs	Employee costs	Repairs	General admin.

figure 8.2 The first page of the cashbook

payments out' column. Subtract the second from the first and you get your current bank balance – positive if you are in credit and negative if you are overdrawn.

If the balance brought forward at 1 April is positive (i.e. you are in credit at the bank) it will go in the first line of the 'Total' column for payments in, which you will learn about in Chapter 15. But if you are overdrawn it goes in as the first line of the 'Payments out'. Enter the date, put 'Balance b/f' (for 'brought forward') in the details, nothing in the 'Cheque number' column and the amount in the 'Total column'.

Figure 8.3, below, shows the payments side of Mr Singh's cashbook although the balance brought forward has now been changed. More columns are now included, in the order set out in Chapter 5 – the last columns, not needed for the entries given, are not shown in order to make the illustration more legible. You can now see a balance brought forward of £2040.53 – this means that Mr Singh was overdrawn by this amount according to his bank statement on 1 June. Because he writes up his cashbook only when he receives the bank statement, he does not have to adjust the opening balance at all. The 'Total' column now includes a figure for the initial overdraft, so it no longer shows the amount that has been spent during the month, it shoes the amount by which Mr Singh would now be overdrawn, given the bank balance at the start of the month, if he had made all these payments out but had paid nothing into the account.

Finally, Figure 8.4 below shows Ben Martin's cashbook, payments side only, written up for the first week of May – this is the information you first saw in Table 4.4, back in Chapter 4.

Mr Martin was in credit, so there is no entry for a balance brought forward. The other entries are as you would expect, with the cash contra being taken to drawings. Looking only at the payments side, it is not easy to understand where the cash contra has come from; in fact, as was explained in Chapter 4, it is there because he has kept some of the cash he took in fares to spend for himself. It is therefore recorded as drawings.

Summary

- Buy a 32 column cashbook.
- Start the year on 1 April unless there is a very good reason for choosing another date.
- Start the month with the balance brought forward if overdrawn.
- Add a column for VAT if registered.
- Remember that the columns and rows should all cross check!

Bank account no 123 456 23   Sort code 22-22-22   June 200X

Date	Payments out	Cheque no.	Total	Cost of sales	Employees	Admin	Motor	Travel	Advertising	Legal/ Prof	Finance	Drawings
1 Jun	Bal b/f		2,040.53	2,040.53								
3 Jun	s/o County Leasing		345.22				345.22					
8 Jun	High St Garrage	234	28.34				28.34					
10 Jun	V G Browns		25.68			25.68						
12 Jun	s/o H Singh		500.00									500.00
14 Jun	Charges		42.30								42.30	
18 Jun	Anytown Courier	235	43.69						43.69			
18 Jun	Smarts	237	692.59	662.59								30.00
21 Jun	DD NICO		28.40									28.40
23 Jun	Jones Plumb.	238	254.00	254.00								
23 Jun	Post Office Counters	239	150.00					150.00				
28 Jun	Print Pronto	241	82.38			82.38						
30 Jun	d/d Magnificent Mutual		100.00									100.00
30 Jun	TOTALS		4333.13	2,040.53	916.59	108.06	523.56		43.69		42.30	658.40

figure 8.3 Hardip Singh's payments page, June

Bank account no 123 456 78   Sort code 33-33-33   April 200X

Date	Payments out	Cheque number	Total	Cost of sales	Admin.	Motor	Travel	Advertising	Drawing
1 May	Cabdrivers Ben.	SO	10.00						10.00
3 May	Freeway C/Card	334	143.80	143.80					
3 May	Taxicab leasing	335	350.00			350.00			
6 May	Yellow Pages	336	140.00					140.00	
7 May	Cash contra		150.00						150.00

(Other unused columns are not shown.)

figure 8.4 Ben Martin's payments out page – May

09

non-allowable expenses

In this chapter you will learn:
- which expenses are not allowable for tax
- what expenses to include in your analysis headings.

Introduction

When discussing the analysis headings in Chapter 5 it was suggested that you should not include any expenses which are disallowable for tax purposes. A few brief pointers, covering some of the key areas that you may come across, were given for each heading. This chapter looks in more detail at the expenses which are not allowable for tax, and also suggests some expenses you should include that you may not have thought of.

Taxation is not the main topic of this book, and you should seek more information on this subject if you are not going to use an accountant. The Inland Revenue have a range of booklets, of which the most important is probably 'Starting your own Business', reference CWL1. This can be obtained from your local tax office. You should also ask them for a copy of 'Helpsheet IR 225 – turnover, allowable expenses, and taxable profit or loss'.

'Wholly and exclusively'

The most important general rule is that an expense can only be allowable for tax if it is incurred 'wholly and exclusively' for the purpose of your business. When this rule is applied strictly it can be harsh. A professional guitarist was refused a deduction for the costs of an operation to correct a problem in his little finger, despite evidence that he had the treatment solely to improve his playing – the court held that since he also played for pleasure, the purpose was partly private and partly business. A female barrister who had to wear black skirts and jackets under her robes when in court, but never wore them anywhere else because she did not like wearing black, was refused a deduction. The court held that one motive for wearing the clothes was common decency – she could not walk down the street dressed only in her underwear!

In practice tax inspectors will often agree to split a payment into part business and part private on an appropriate basis, but you should be careful about admitting that there is any private element to an expense, since strictly this disbars it from being tax allowable.

'Revenue, not capital'

Another key concept is that the expense must be a revenue expense, and not a capital purchase. Some capital expenditure, mainly that on plant and machinery (including motor cars), gets a separate relief called **capital allowances**. Details of how to record the purchase of capital equipment are included in the next chapter, and the calculation of capital allowances is also dealt with briefly. However, some capital expenditure gets no relief at all. The purchase of an office building or a shop, for example, cannot be claimed against tax.

This concept gives rise to some peculiar decisions. If a boiler and chimney are part of a factory, and they are knocked down and rebuilt, still as part of the same factory, that is probably a repair to the factory and therefore allowable as a revenue expense. However, if a factory has a separate building housing the boiler and chimney which is completely demolished and a new one built, that is probably a capital expense.

Franchise businesses can cause problems. A fee for initial training is often seen as a capital expense, because it puts you in a position to carry out your business rather than keeping you up to date to continue it. For the same reason, a fee for training that keeps you up to date will normally be allowable against tax. A fee paid simply as a one-off payment to use the franchise name may well be capital, whereas payment of an ongoing annual fee is probably revenue, and allowable. If you are intending to set up a franchise business you should get clear written advice from the franchisor of any negotiations they have had with the Inland Revenue on the allowability of the charges they make.

These two rules – 'wholly and exclusively' and 'revenue not capital' – are the main source of tax disallowances. Discussed below are several particular areas in which the operation of one or the other of these rules causes problems.

Loans

The interest charged on a loan is a revenue expense, and allowable for tax purposes. The capital repayments are not.

Leases and hire purchase

If a piece of equipment is provided to you on lease, so that you never actually own it, the full expense is normally allowable in your accounts against tax. This remains true even if the rental reduces to a very low figure after a fixed period, say three or five years, although if the period when the 'full-price' rental is paid is significantly less than the useful life of the asset, the Inspector of Taxes may want to make an adjustment. A normal period of three to five years for equipment such as motor cars or computers should not cause a problem.

If the contract gives you the right to purchase the asset, such as in a hire purchase or some lease purchase arrangements, then for tax purposes you are treated as if you own the asset from the start, and the payments under the contract are a combination of loan repayments and finance – the former being non-allowable and the latter allowable.

Motor expenses

The Inland Revenue will allow you to claim a poportion of total motor expenses which matches the business mileage. So if your total mileage is 10,000 a year and 8,000 of that is on business, you can claim 80% of your total motor expenses. This is one area where it IS a good idea to record ALL the expenses and enter them onto the tax return and then to enter the amount disallowed (20% in this example) into the box for disallowable expenses – if you do not, the inspector is likely to ask whether you have made a disallowance.

The ideal way to document the amount of business mileage is to log every journey. In practice the inspector will accept that most taxpayers do not do so, and will accept an estimate. However, it is useful to keep a log for a representative period if possible (a month, say) as evidence of how the appropriate percentages were arrived at.

If the business has a turnover of less than the current VAT limit, it is possible to avoid recording the details of motor expenses, and just to claim a mileage allowance. If you want to do this, you should write to your Tax Inspector and ask for advice on the latest allowances and how to apply them. In your business records, you would no longer include any motor expenses at all – you would pay them privately or treat them as drawings.

When you came to transfer the figures to your tax return, you would calculate the amount for motor expenses from the business miles done and the appropriate mileage allowance for your car. This can be a tax-efficient way of claiming motor expenses, particularly if your car is second-hand, because the rates of depreciation assumed in the allowances are based on a new car. However in this case you would need to log at least your business mileage accurately.

Subscriptions

Even if you find them useful for business purposes, the Inland Revenue will normally disallow subscriptions for golf club membership, Rotary clubs etc. Membership of professional and trade bodies is normally allowed.

Entertainment

Entertainment expenditure, except for staff entertainment, is not allowable at all. You may have heard that it is allowable if you are entertaining foreign customers; this used to be true but it has been abolished. This includes 'business lunches' and any other similar expenses.

Entertaining your staff will be tax deductible for you, but may mean that they get a tax bill on the benefit in kind. The main exception to this is the reasonable costs of a staff Christmas party – you can deduct this for tax purposes and there will be no tax charged on the staff members.

Hotels and subsistence

If you stay away overnight on business you can claim the cost of the overnight accommodation and the cost of your meals. If you do not stay overnight, you cannot normally claim the cost of your meals, even if you have been out on a business trip all day and were therefore forced to eat your meals away from home.

Travel

Travel from your place of business to a customer, client etc. is allowable, even if your place of business is your home. Travel from home to your place of business is not allowable. You can have arguments with the Inland Revenue when you work for substantial periods at a client's premises – they may try to disallow the cost of travelling there from your home. You should ensure that you can prove your business is operated from home – that you do work there whenever you can, that you store equipment there, that you write out from home looking for further work, and of course that your accounting books and records are at home and are written up there.

Allowable expenses

Having emphasised above the sort of expenses which are probably not allowable, here are some that you might not have thought of which may be allowable.

Newspapers, magazines etc. may be allowable on the basis that they are used for business research. Computer magazines, in particular, may fall into this category if you use a computer for business.

Special protective clothing may be allowable as an expense, although the Inland Revenue will not normally allow the costs of normal day-to-day clothing.

Use of home – if you run your business from home, some of the expenses of running the home are allowable. If you spend a lot of time at home, working say in the spare bedroom, you may want to claim say a sixth of all the rent, light, heat, council tax bills etc. If you are based at home but spend most of your time travelling or at clients' premises, you may simply estimate your expense by claiming a few pounds a week.

In the examples used in this book, Grace Morris would claim at least half of the rent, light, heat etc. of the property, since they live upstairs and the shop premises are downstairs. She might argue for a higher percentage on the grounds that the shop probably uses more electricity than the flat. Ben Martin would be unwise to try to claim more than a few pounds a week, since realistically he spends most of his working time away from home. However, he writes up his books and records there, keeps his taxi in the garage overnight, and no doubt works on it at weekends, so a few pounds a week is reasonable. If Hardip Singh uses his spare bedroom as an office and his garage is normally full of building materials, he might want to claim say a fifth of his heat and light etc. – although the Tax Inspector might challenge this on the grounds that he spends most of his time out at the sites where he is working.

10

purchase of equipment

In this chapter you will learn:
- how to record purchases of equipment
- how to calculate the capital allowances on equipment
- the special rules for purchasing cars.

Scope of this chapter

You will know from reading the last chapter that capital expenditure is not tax allowable in the way that revenue expenses are. However, the purchase of equipment such as shop-fittings, machinery, cars, vans etc. does get tax relief, under the separate system of capital allowances. When you get your tax return, you will find that the pages dealing with self-employment have boxes for you to fill in to calculate your profit before allowances, and then a separate set of boxes for showing the capital allowances that are due to you.

Unfortunately the return does not include a working sheet for calculating capital allowances, and the tax return guide for the self-employment schedule does not go into any details. You need to ask for 'Helpsheet 226 – Capital allowances and balancing charges', which does give an explanation of how to do the calculations, and gives a few examples.

This chapter takes you through the complete process of recording purchases of equipment and then at the end of the year calculating the capital allowances on them, covering normal business plant and machinery, and also the special rules for motor cars. However, the subject of capital allowances is a complicated one, and can only be covered in outline here. If you use an accountant to prepare your final accounts and tax return, then all you will need to do is to follow the instructions set out in the first three paragraphs of the section on *Recording transactions*, below. If you do not use an accountant, read through this chapter and the Inland Revenue helpsheet very carefully. If you are in any doubt, contact your local Inland Revenue Tax Enquiry Centre for help. It is probably best to do this at the end of the year, when you can go in with your books and records and work through the figures with a member of the Inland Revenue staff.

Recording transactions

There is nothing unusual about the way that purchases of equipment are recorded when they are bought outright. The amount paid is shown in the 'Total' column, and is then also included in the 'Purchase of equipment' column.

Equally there is no problem when equipment is taken on a lease, where you have no right to purchase it – as explained in the last chapter this is simply treated as a business expense, and included in other finance charges, or in motor expenses if they relate to a car. However, leasing is not always the most appropriate option, and is not normally suitable if you are not VAT-registered.

The other two possibilities are that the equipment is bought on instalments through a hire purchase or lease purchase arrangement; or that a loan is taken out to repay it. These are both more complicated to handle, and if you are using an accountant it may be best simply to include the payments in the purchase of equipment column and let your accountant sort them out. However, if you are handling your own affairs, you have to make the necessary adjustments.

The best way to deal with it, although it is unorthodox in accounting terms, is to record it as two contra entries: one as the purchase of the asset for the full cash price; the other as capital introduced into the business. What this says is that you as the business owner have put the money into the business in order to buy the asset. The fact that you did it by borrowing the money does not change this. As a result, the capital repayments each month or quarter go to drawings. The interest element goes to other finance charges, and is an allowable expense.

Working out the amount of the payment which is interest can be difficult, and you should get the help of the lender to do this for you when you take out the finance. Failing that, a simple but not entirely accurate approach is to divide the total amount borrowed by the number of payments you will make, and treat that much each month as a capital repayment and the rest as interest. This understates the true interest in the early years and overstates it in later years, so you should make a note on your tax return telling the Inspector what you have done.

Example

Grace Morris buys a new freezer for the shop for £3,000. She pays for it in twelve instalments of £300 each. Because it is a short credit agreement, she decides to use the simple calculation above to decide how much of each payment is capital.

$3,000 \div 12 = 250.$

Therefore £250 of each repayment is capital and £50 is interest.

Figure 10.1 shows two entries in her cashbook. The first is the entry for the initial purchase and the loan. There is no cheque number, because she has not had to pay out the £3,000 in reality as she has arranged finance for it. So the £3,000 expenditure is

Date	Payments out	Total	Equipment	Drawings	Finance	Date	Payments in	Total	Capital int.
1 XX	Freezer (paid by loan)	3,000.00	3,000.00			1XX	Contra for freezer loan	3,000.00	3,000.00
Mth 1	Repayment	300.00		250.00	50.00				

figure 10.1 Grace Morris – purchase of freezer

Date	Payments out	Total	Equipment	Drawings	Finance	Date	Payments in	Total	Capital int.
1 XX	Freezer (paid by loan)	3,000.00	3,000.00			1XX	Contra for freezer loan	3,000.00	3,000.00
Mth 1	Repayment	300.00		250.00	50.00				
Mth 2	Repayment	300.00		250.00	50.00				
Mth 3	Repayment	300.00		250.00	50.00				
Mth 4	Repayment	300.00		250.00	50.00				
Mth 5	Repayment	300.00		250.00	50.00				
Mth 6	Repayment	300.00		250.00	50.00				
Mth 7	Repayment	300.00		250.00	50.00				
Mth 8	Repayment	300.00		250.00	50.00				
Mth 9	Repayment	300.00		250.00	50.00				
Mth 10	Repayment	300.00		250.00	50.00				
Mth 11	Repayment	300.00		250.00	50.00				
Mth 12	Repayment	300.00		250.00	50.00				
TOTAL		6,600.00	3,000.00	3,000.00	600.00			3,000.00	3,000.00

figure 10.2 Grace Morris – purchase of freezer

a contra entry with a corresponding entry in receipts as capital introduced. The subject of capital introduced is dealt with in more detail in Chapter 16. The net effect is to leave the bank balance unchanged (which is as it should be, since no money has actually gone out at this point), but the acquisition of the freezer at the cash price of £3,000 is now reflected in the books.

The second entry is one of the twelve monthly payments. Of the £300 total paid each month, £250 goes to drawings. You will find in Chapter 16 that capital introduced is simply the opposite of drawings – it is money put into the business rather than money taken out. Just as the initial loan was taken to capital introduced, so the repayments are taken to drawings. The remaining £50 is recorded as an interest payment, which is an allowable expense.

It may be easier to understand how this works if you look at Figure 10.2. This shows in summary form all the entries connected with the purchase of the freezer – the initial contra entries and then the twelve monthly credit instalment payments, which reflect the actual payments out of the bank account. Look at the totals at the bottom of the analysis. There is £3,000 in total for purchase of equipment, which correctly records the cash price of the freezer, and is not allowable for tax. There is £600 in interest, which is the actual amount of interest she has paid – her total payments are £300 × 12 = £3,600. And finally there are two sums of £3,000, one in drawings and one in capital introduced. These just say that she took £3,000 out of the business and put £3,000 into it. They offset each other, and have no net effect on the accounts.

Receipts from sales of equipment are simply recorded as a negative expense – subtracted from the figures on the payments side of the book. However, if you are preparing full accounts see the more detailed explanation in Appendix 2.

Capital allowance calculations

The rules for capital allowances have been changing in recent years, with several temporary schemes offering 40% or even 100% allowances in the year that the expenditure is incurred. You need to check the information in the current helpsheet very carefully to see whether any such allowances are available to you for the current year. The examples below assume that they are not.

At the end of the year, you will add up all the figures in the 'Purchase of equipment' column, and come to a total. This is the cash price of the equipment you have acquired in the year, even if some of it still has not been paid for in full. Next, you need to take out of this the price of any motor cars, unless they are used for a trade, short-term hire or for passenger carriage.

You add what is left to the balance of unrelieved expenditure from earlier years – this is known as the **pool**. Next you subtract the amount you received from the sale of assets. Finally, you calculate 25% of the remainder, known as the **writing down allowance**. These are the capital allowances you are claiming on ordinary plant and equipment, and this figure goes onto your tax return, as explained in the helpsheet. The remaining 75% is the pool that you carry forward to the following year.

Example

Hardip Singh started the year with a pool of unrelieved expenditure on equipment totalling £8,600. During the year he bought a cement mixer for £300 and a trailer for £100. He sold a van for £1,000 (vans are included in the pool, provided they are of a type primarily for carrying goods).

Figure 10.3 shows how he calculates his capital allowances on the pool. The allowances to be entered into his tax return are £2,000.

Pool brought forward	8600
Purchases	400
	9000
Sales	(1000)
	8000
Capital allowances@25%	(2000)
Pool carried forward	6000

figure 10.3 Hardip Singh – capital allowances

Motor cars are more complicated. In practice, virtually every small business has to calculate the capital allowances for each car separately, because all the cars are almost invariably used partially for private purposes as well as business, or would have cost more than £12,000 new (even if bought second-hand). If you have more than one car which is *not* covered by either of those provisions you will need to ask the Inland Revenue to help you with the calculation.

Each car is treated as a separate pool of expenditure. Each year, you deduct 25% to claim as allowances, and carry the balance forward. There are, however, some particular points to note.

Notes

1 If the balance of expenditure brought forward on any one car is more than £12,000, you do not calculate 25% of it: you simply take £3,000 as the capital allowance.

2 If the car is used for personal as well as business use, then after you have completed the calculation and reached the new balance of expenditure to carry forward, you have to deduct an appropriate percentage from the capital allowance you were going to claim. The result of this is that eventually you only get to claim the percentage of the cost of the car that reflects your business use.

3 If the car is sold during the year, you do not calculate the 25% figure. Instead you simply deduct the proceeds of the sale from the remaining balance. If the result is a negative figure, this is a balancing charge, and has to be reported on your tax return – this will *increase* the amount on which you have to pay tax. If, as is more normal, there is still a balance of unrelieved expenditure, this is a balancing allowance and also has to be reported on the tax return but it will reduce the amount on which you pay tax.

4 If you have chosen to claim mileage allowance rather than recording your motor expenses in full, this includes an amount for depreciation, and no capital allowances are due.

Example

Grace Morris has an estate car which she bought some years ago. At the beginning of the year the unrelieved expenditure on it was £2,000. Although she uses it mainly for carrying goods from the Cash & Carry, it is a motor car for capital allowance purposes, because it was constructed mainly for carrying passengers. During the year she sells the estate car for £1,000 and buys another one for £10,000. Her private mileage is 10% of her total mileage.

Figure 10.4, below, shows how the allowances are calculated. Note that, for both the balancing allowance and the writing-down allowance on the new vehicle, the 10% private usage deduction is the last part of the calculation.

	Old car	New car	Allowances
Pool brought forward	2000		
Sale in year	(1000)		
Balancing allowance	(1000)		1000
Purchase		10000	
Writing-down allowance		(2500)	2500
10% private use			(350)
Poll c/f	—	7500	
Allowances given			3150

figure10.4 Grace Morris – capital allowances on car

Summary

If you have worked through the chapter to here, you will not need to be told that handling your own capital allowance claim is complicated. The main point to bear in mind is that you need to be able to tell either your accountant or the Inland Revenue about:

- the equipment you have acquired during the year, and the cash price of it
- the equipment you have sold during the year and what you received for the sale
- the interest element of any repayments you have made.

Provided you can do this, even if you want to handle your own affairs, it should be possible to get help from an Inland Revenue Tax Enquiry Centre to work out the necessary figures.

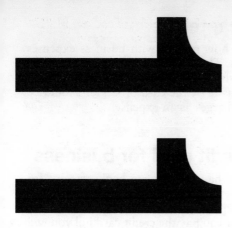

11

credit cards

In this chapter you will learn:
- how to use a credit card for business
- how to deal with business expenses charged to your credit card
- how to file your credit card transactions.

Scope of this chapter

The details below explain how to deal with business expenses charged to your credit card. They do not deal with the handling of credit card receipts, which should be handled as cheque receipts, and the charges made by the card processor should be included in other finance charges as an expense.

How to use a credit card for business

In the same way that you have a separate bank account for business, it is useful to have one or more credit or charge cards solely for your business expenditure. If you mix personal and business expenditure, when you pay the credit card bill you will have to charge some of it to drawings. You will also probably not be able to charge any interest against tax, and certainly will not be able to charge the annual fee against tax, since the expenditure will not be wholly for business purposes.

Having said that, it is a good idea to pay off the credit card bill in full every month, rather than taking advantage of the credit facilities. In part this is for the normal reason that interest charges on a credit card are far higher than most other forms of finance, but it is also because it causes difficulties in recording the transaction.

Bill paid in full

Where the bill is paid in full, there is little difficulty in recording it. It is simply a single payment for a number of different expenses, so the amount paid goes in the 'Total' column and is then analysed in the analysis columns.

When the cashbook entry is to be made, mark each item on the credit card statement according to the category of expenditure (cost of sales, motor expenses, general administrative expenses etc.) into which it falls. If there are any private expenses, classify them as drawings. Then at the bottom of the bill, calculate subtotals for each of these categories, and check that when you add up the subtotals you get back to the total amount paid. These subtotals are the figures you enter into the analysis columns.

Example

Ben Martin's Visa bill records the following expenditure:

1 Two purchases of diesel from High Road garage, which will not accept his normal fuel charge card
2 Purchase of a cashbook and two lever-arch files for his accounts
3 Payment for a business advertisement in the local paper
4 The cost of some business cards he had printed
5 The deposit on the family's summer holiday

Figure 11.1 shows how the bill looked, and his calculation of the subtotals. Figure 11.2 then shows how they were entered in the cashbook when he paid the bill.

When only part of the bill is paid off

Strictly speaking, the correct way to handle this is to open a new cashbook that records only the credit card payments, and to show payments from the bank account as movements between the two accounts. But this is too complicated for a small business, so it is suggested that you use a similar approach to that for purchase of equipment on credit.

Enter the transaction on the payments side of the cashbook exactly as you would if you had paid it off in full. Then, on the receipts side, show a contra entry as capital introduced for the amount that you didn't pay off. When in a subsequent month all or part of the balance is paid off, treat the excess payment over and above the amount charged to the card during that month as drawings.

Example

The facts in Figure 11.3 below are exactly as for Figure 11.2, except that Ben Martin only paid £100 of the bill. You can see that the difference between the amount charged in the payments side and the contra entry on the receipts side of the cashbook is £100.

Next month he charges the following to his credit card.

1 Two more bills for fuel from the garage
2 A subscription to *Black Taxi Monthly*

VISA

Mr B Martin
1 The Square
Histown
HH1 1HH

23.6.200X

26.5	High Road garage	*Cost of Sales*	16.45
3.6	The Stationery Shop	*Admin.*	14.23
4.6	High Road garage	*Cost of Sales*	19.56
5.6	The Histown Advertiser	*Advertising*	45.98
12.6	Pronto Printo	*Admin.*	32.56
18.6	Sunny Days Holiday Co	*Drawings*	90.00
TOTAL			218.78

Cost of Sales	*Admin.*	*Advertising*	*Drawings*
16.45	14.23	45.98	90.00
19.56	32.56		
36.01	46.79	45.98	90.00

£ 218.78

Paid in full 2/7

348

figure 11.1 Ben Martin's Visa bill

Date	Payments out	Ch no	Total	Cost of Sales	Administration	Advertising	Drawings
2/7	Visa	348	218.78	36.01	46.79	45.98	90.00

figure 11.2 entry in Ben Martin's cash book for Visa bill

He pays off the whole of the balance when the bill arrives. His bill and the calculations he makes on it are shown in Figure 11.4 below. The interest has all been taken to drawings, rather than bothering to try to allocate it between the separate purchases. Note that the balance brought forward (which is the same as the amount shown as capital introduced in last month's entry) is treated as drawings.

Figure 11.5 repeats the cashbook entry shown in Figure 11.3, then adds the entry for the following month. The figures have then been totalled, and the amount shown as capital introduced deducted from the drawings. If you compare this with the transactions for the two months you will find that they are now all accurately recorded. The figure for drawings, in particular, is now made up of the deposit on the family holiday and the interest charge.

Filing

The invoices and receipts for the credit card purchases should be kept separately. It is a good idea to punch holes in an A4 envelope and keep this at the front of your lever-arch folder for them. Once the credit card bill arrives, the invoices and receipts are checked off against it, then stapled to the back of the bill for filing. The cheque number and date of payment are written on the front of the credit card statement before it is filed in the usual way, but you should write the amount of the payment (or 'paid in full') on the front of the statement as well.

Notes on timing

In theory, paying for something by credit card is the same as paying for it by cash or cheque – you have incurred the expense on the day that you sign the credit card voucher. In practice, this system means that you only record the expense as having occurred in the month when the bill is paid, rather than the month when the transaction happened. Generally this does not cause a problem, but in some situations it can.

1 **If you miss a payment completely**   Most credit and charge cards insist on at least some payment being made each month, but if you forget they will normally carry the balance forward to the next bill (whilst adding interest and in some cases a late payment charge, of course). If you do

(Payments side)

Date	Payments out	Ch no	Total	Cost of Sales	Administration	Advertising	Drawings
2/7	Visa	348	218.78	36.01	46.79	45.98	90.00

(Receipts side)

Date	Payments in		Total	Sales	Capital introduced
2/7	Visa (contra)		118.78		118.78

figure 11.3 entry in Ben Martin's cashbook for part payment of Visa bill

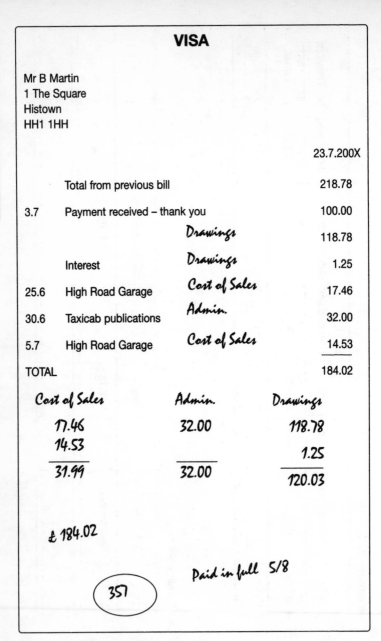

figure 11.4 Ben Martin's second Visa bill

(Payments side)

Date	Payments out	Ch no	Total	Cost of Sales	Administration	Advertising	Drawings
2/7	Visa	348	218.78	36.01	46.79	45.98	90.00
5/8	Visa	357	184.02	31.99	32.00		120.03
TOTALS			402.80	68.00	78.79	45.98	210.03
Deduct capital introduced			118.78				118.78
			284.02				91.25

(Receipts side)

Date	Payments in		Total	Sales	Capital introduced
2/7	Visa (contra)		118.78		118.78

figure 11.5 entries in Ben Martin's cash book after payment of second bill

not make an entry in your books when you miss a payment like this, it is easy to forget about the expenses recorded on the previous statement and fail to record them under the correct categories. If you have missed a payment, treat it as a bill which was not paid in full. Enter it on the payments side as if it had been paid in full, and then show the same amount on the receipts side as capital introduced.

2 **At the end of the year**   If you have an expense in the last month of the year and charge it to your credit card, it is likely that it will not be paid until the new business year has started. This means that you will have to pay more tax for the year which has just ended, and less for the year just starting. Obviously it would be better to have the expense deducted in the earliest year possible.

If you want to do this you can make an adjustment for the amounts due as a creditor – see Chapter 22. However, if you start to do this you must do it consistently, which means that as well as increasing expenses for the bill paid after the end of this business year, you will have to reduce them for the bill included in the first month of this year, which actually related to the last month of the previous year. In practice, provided the amounts are small compared to the total expenses of the business, it is unlikely that the Inland Revenue will raise an objection if you consistently record the expense as occurring in the month the bill is paid.

3 **At the end of a VAT quarter**   VAT is dealt with in full in Chapter 18, but the principle here is the same as for the year end – you will be getting relief for VAT paid in the quarter when the credit card bill is paid, not the one in which the expense was incurred. Again, if you are going to make an adjustment you would have to do so consistently; normally it is just not worthwhile. Penalties for under-declarations are mainly incurred when amounts of £1,000 or more of VAT have been included in the wrong quarter, so the slight timing difference caused by credit card payments should not be a problem.

Summary

- Pay off credit card bills in full each month if you can.
- If you cannot, treat the payment in the same way as purchases of equipment on credit.
- Make sure you record the expenses if you miss a payment.
- Make adjustments if needed for timing differences.

12 petty cash

In this chapter you will learn:
- three methods for dealing with petty cash
- the advantages and disadvantages of each method.

The key feature of this book-keeping system is that it starts from the bank statements. As a result, it is essential that sooner or later all transactions are reflected in the bank account.

However, inevitably some expenses have to be paid in cash. You will find – typically – that you pay in cash for small items of stationery, taxi fares and so on. How are these going to be reflected through the bank account? There are two ways you can do this effectively, both based on the idea that you accumulate petty cash receipts and from time to time write a cheque to cover the accumulated cost. You then treat the cheque in the same way as the one paying off your credit card – split the total among the relevant categories of expenditure.

The real question is how methodical you are going to be about your petty cash. Three methods are set out below in increasing order of formality. However the second method, although probably the most commonly used, is not recommended for use with this book-keeping system. The reason is that the cheque payment cannot be accurately analysed into the appropriate categories of expenditure.

Cheque reimbursement

The simplest approach is not to keep any sort of petty cash box or cash that is earmarked for business expenses. When you need to pay cash you use your own money, but you keep the receipts carefully.

Every so often, you sort the receipts out into the categories of expenditure used in your cashbook. Most of them are likely to be general administrative expenses or travel expenses, but there may be some others. Use a sheet of A4 paper to list out the receipts for each category and add up the amounts to get to separate subtotals. Then add these together to get the total for which the cheque is made out. You can either make the cheque out for cash, and put this in your pocket, or you can pay it into your personal bank account. In either case, the subtotals are the entries for the analysis columns.

Example

Ben Martin is going through his petty cash receipts. He has receipts for a mapbook, a can of de-icer, a B&B when he had a long trip and could not get back that night, a pen and a book of stamps. Figure 12.1 shows how he writes these up on a sheet of

A4 paper, and Figure 12.2 shows how he enters them into his cashbook. He pays the cheque into his private bank account.

```
    Motor Expenses:
    7/5    De-icer                      3.49
    1/6    Mapbook                      4.99
                                        8.48

    Administration Expenses
    28/6   Pen                          1.19
    28/6   Stamps                       2.60
                                        3.79

    Travel Expenses
    2/5    Clearview B  B, Hastings     23.00

    Total                               35.27

    Ch. no. 362  10.7
```

figure 12.1 Ben Martin's petty cash list

Date	Payments out	Cheque no	Total	Cost of sales	Motor exes.	Admin	Travel
10.7	Petty cash	362	35.27		8.48	3.79	23.00

figure 12.2 Ben Martin's cashbook record of petty cash

Advantages and disadvantages

The great advantage of this system is that it has no formality about it. All you have to do is to sit down every so often and write up the receipts. The disadvantages are also to do with this informality. It is easy, over the weeks, to lose the receipts or forget what they were for. If you have to spend a lot in cash the system will soon become unwieldy. And perhaps most importantly of all, if you do not get a receipt, you are unlikely to remember to claim for it. This could be particularly problematic for someone like Mr Martin, as he has probably paid quite a lot of cash into parking meters, toll fees for bridges and tunnels etc.

Simple petty cash box

The next stage up is to have a petty cash box, and to draw a certain amount in petty cash to be kept in it – say £100. Whenever you pay for something in cash, as soon as you get back home or to your business premises, you put the receipt into the box and take out the amount of cash you have spent. If you do not get a receipt you write out a slip which explains what the payment is for. Petty cash slips are sold at stationers, although there is no reason why you should not just use scrap paper for this.

When the amount of cash is getting low, a cheque is written for a further £100 to top it up. This is the flaw in this way of dealing with petty cash, and the reason why it cannot be used with this book-keeping system. If the cash in the box is down to say £10, there should be £90 of petty cash receipts in it. However, the cheque that is being written is for £100, so the amounts charged to each category of expense will not match up to the total.

The change that is needed should be obvious – instead of writing a cheque for the full £100, write a cheque for £90 instead. This is the basis of the third, and best, system for petty cash.

Imprest petty cash system

This petty cash system is so well known that it has a name – the **imprest system**. *Imprest* is an archaic word meaning a loan. It works in exactly the same way as the second system above, except that when the cash is topped up again it is brought back up to the preset amount, rather than with a round sum.

Example

Hardip Singh operates an imprest petty cash system, with £300 in his petty cash box. Whenever he pays for something in cash, he puts the receipt or a petty cash voucher for it into the cash box and takes out the corresponding amount of money. At the end of each week he checks that it balances. With an imprest system, the total of the cash left in the box and the amounts shown on the receipts that are in it should always be the same as the amount chosen, £300 in this case. Whenever the balance falls below £100 he writes up the petty cash receipts and draws out a cheque to bring the amount back up to £300.

Figure 12.3 shows his calculations. Whilst there was only £90 in the box, the receipts total £205. Mr Singh does not know what has happened to the £5, but since he cannot show what business expense it was used for, he has to treat it as drawings. The entry made in his cashbook is shown in Figure 12.4.

Advantages and disadvantages

The advantages of this system are self-evident. At any time, the receipts and the cash can be added together to see if they still equal the imprest amount – if this is done regularly there is a better chance of remembering when and for what the missing amount was taken. Because the cheque is for the same amount as the total petty cash slips, it can be accurately analysed in the cashbook entry.

Cost of Sales		
1.9	Homeways Hardware	35.00
10.9	Homeways Hardware	10.00
12.9	Rubbish clearance	40.00
		85.00
Motor Expenses		
4.9	High St Garage	25.00
3.10	Benfords Auto Accessories	35.00
		60.00
Travel Expenses		
12.9	2 nights B B (castle view) Croydon	60.00
		205.00
Cash in box		90.00
		295.00
Drawings?		5.00
483 15/10 £210		300.00

figure 12.3 Hardip Singh's petty cash list

Date	Payments out	Ch no	Total	Cost of Sales	Motor exp.	Travel exp.	Drawings
15/10	Petty Cash	483	210.00	85.00	60.00	60.00	5.00

figure 12.4 Hardip Singh's cashbook

The only disadvantage is the formality of it, and the necessity for the petty cash slips to be written up and checked against the cash before more petty cash is drawn from the bank. This is, however, a minor inconvenience compared to the advantages it gives. Unless cash purchases form an extremely minor expense, both in relative and absolute terms, it is generally worthwhile using an imprest petty cash system.

Summary

Ideally use an imprest petty cash system, topping the petty cash float back up to a set level. If this is not possible, keep the receipts and write a cheque for the total from business to private account.

13

receipts – filing

In this chapter you will learn:
- how to file invoices and other paperwork to back up your accounting records
- different systems for cash- or credit-based businesses.

In the past eight chapters we have concentrated on how to record expenses. In the next four chapters we look at receipts. Less space is devoted to receipts because in general they are easier to record. Whilst it is necessary to ensure that expenses are analysed correctly among the different categories, there are really only two reasons why money is paid into the business bank account. The first is that it is business income; the second is that it comes from some other sort of funds. For the purposes of this system, any money coming into the business which is not business income is treated (initially at least) as **capital introduced**, and the recording of it is dealt with in detail in Chapter 16.

Corresponding to Chapters 6–8 on payments, there are now three chapters dealing with receipts in general. This chapter considers the filing of invoices and other paperwork to back up the accounting records, Chapter 14 looks at the entries made in the bank paying-in book, and Chapter 15 explains how the cashbook is to be completed.

Cash or credit?

Unlike the system for filing bills received, there are two different situations to be considered when looking at receipts. The business may be primarily one that is run on credit, where invoices are issued and paid after some delay by customers or clients. Alternatively, it may be a business where goods or services are normally paid for at the time they are purchased. Even if some payments are made by cheque or credit card, this is known as a **cash** business. The considerations are different for each of these types of business.

In a credit-based business there are generally fewer transactions in total. Hardip Singh might only have fifty customers in a year; Grace Morris would have that many in a day. Credit bills are generally paid by cheque, so that the individual payment will at some point be entered onto a paying-in slip, and can be connected back to the invoice. In a cash-based business, even if some payments are made by cheque, it is unlikely that it will be possible to identify individual purchases separately. The only realistic approach is to try to set reasonable points at which the takings are totalled – generally daily.

Finally, there is a difference in the amount of attention that different types of business can expect from the Inland Revenue and Customs & Excise. It is generally easier to check whether a credit business has under-declared its takings than a cash-based one, because the cheques have to be paid into a bank account somewhere. Whilst it is possible to run a completely separate set of invoices, bank account and purchases which the tax inspector never sees, it is difficult. On the other hand, it seems easy to take cash out of the till before it is entered into the books.

Because of this concern, both the Inland Revenue and Customs & Excise have developed sophisticated methods for calculating the likely gross profit of typical cash businesses, and it would be an unwise proprietor who tried to dupe them. However, what is easy for a proprietor is also easy for staff, and there are obvious benefits in using appropriate technology such as electronic tills in order to minimise the possibility of fraud or error.

Credit-based business

The filing required for a credit-based business will be reminiscent of that for purchases. An invoice has to be prepared for each job done. One of the easiest ways of doing this is to use a pre-numbered **duplicate invoice book**, which is sold by most stationers. Using a sheet of carbon paper, as each invoice is written out a duplicate is left behind in the book. If a more professional look is required, pre-printed two-part forms can be purchased or printed to order on carbonless paper, and filled in using a typewriter. Alternatively, invoices can be produced on a computer. Two copies need to be printed off.

The two essentials about an invoicing system are that the invoices are numbered and that a duplicate is kept. The numbering ensures that no invoice is lost, and assures the Inland Revenue that none has been deliberately concealed. The duplicates give you a system for chasing up unpaid bills.

If the number of invoices issued is quite large – say more than ten a week – it may be appropriate to use pre-printed forms, rather than a duplicate book, and file the copies in the same way as bills paid. You would use another lever-arch file with a divider card and file the invoices still unpaid above the divider card in issue order. When the invoice was paid you would write the date of payment on it and move it below the divider card.

However, for most businesses it is sufficient simply to keep a file of the copy invoices in issue order. When the invoice is paid you write the date of payment on it.

Credit management

Apart from recording the income of the business, the invoices have an essential role to play in credit management. In Chapter 6 on payment of bills you were encouraged to take advantage of the credit terms that your suppliers offered. However, when looking at the money owed to you, it is essential that you encourage your customers to pay up promptly, and that you follow them up more and more vigorously as debts get older.

Your invoices should state the time when you expect to be paid – this may be within seven days, two weeks or a month; it is rarely longer. Whilst you can issue a statement before that time has expired, you obviously cannot chase payment aggressively. Once the time limit has expired without payment, you may want to send out a reminder that payment is **overdue**. If this does not result in payment you will probably need to make personal contact by telephone.

Whilst experience varies from business to business, most would expect to get paid within 30 to 60 days of issuing the invoice. An invoice outstanding for more than 90 days without good reason is often a trigger for enforcement action: either by instructing solicitors or a debt collection agency, or by personally taking out a summons in the county court. The latter is not expensive or difficult, and a letter saying that such a summons will be issued without further warning if payment is not received in seven days will normally result in a cheque by return. Just as your creditors may start to add statutory interest and charges to overdue invoices, you may do the same to your debtors. However, as previously mentioned, at present these provisions seem to be little used, and it may be counter-productive for future sales.

Clearly this involves a careful review of the invoices, either *ad hoc* when a new invoice is filled in or at a specified time every week or two. If you use loose copies of the invoices filed separately when paid or unpaid it should be easy to identify the old ones. In a pre-printed duplicate book you have to check carefully that you have not missed any very old invoices still unpaid when all those around them have been. It can be useful to keep your place by putting a bulldog clip over the pages at the back of the book when all the invoices underneath the top one are paid, so that you only have to flick through the remaining pages.

Make notes on the invoice duplicates to remind you what you have done and when you did it, making sure that you can distinguish them easily from the note that an invoice is paid.

Example

Mr Singh uses a pre-printed duplicate book for invoices, and has a similar one for issuing statements. He normally only issues statements after payment is overdue, and gives people fourteen days to pay. In practice he finds most people pay between a month and six weeks after he bills them.

On 1 August he writes out an invoice for the latest job, billing Mr Davis for £400 for work on his roof. Having written this out and put the top copy in an envelope to be posted to Mr Davis, he looks through the duplicates. Two of the latest invoices are unpaid, but are still recent. An invoice for Mr Matthews is dated 7 July and has not been paid, so he writes out a statement and posts it to him, noting on the duplicate that he has done so. Going further back through the book, all the other bills have been paid except for one to Mrs Jones, dated 14 June. A statement had been sent to her on 10 July. He rings Mrs Jones to remind her that payment of the bill is now long overdue, and is promised that the cheque will be in the post the following morning. He notes this on the copy invoice, and puts a note in his desk diary for a week's time to ring again if the cheque has not been received. See Figure 13.1 for copies of all these invoices as they appear after he has finished.

Cash businesses

There is one very important principle for cash-based businesses – never, ever take cash out of the till without leaving a note that this has been done, so that it can either be repaid or accounted for by a contra entry. Indeed, for preference do not take money out of the till at all – use a petty cash box. This is one of the most common reasons for cash businesses under-declaring their profits, either deliberately or accidentally, and will always be a question raised in a tax investigation.

The chances of doing this can be reduced by using an electronic till that provides you with a printed total for the day of the cash, cheques and credit card receipts that should be in the till – this would be an ideal solution for Grace Morris. The best form of

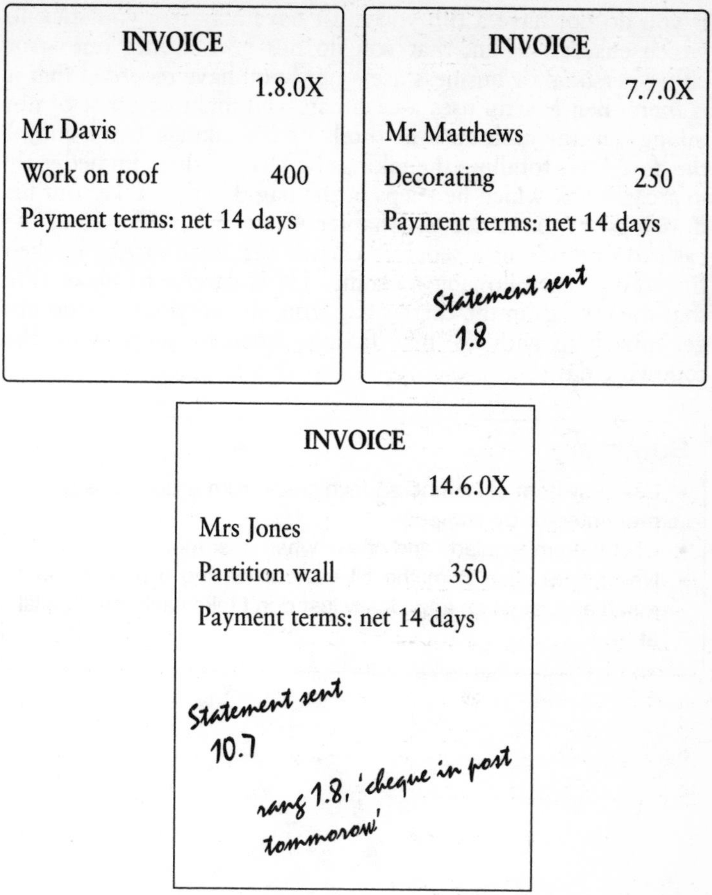

INVOICE

1.8.0X

Mr Davis

Work on roof   400

Payment terms: net 14 days

INVOICE

7.7.0X

Mr Matthews

Decorating   250

Payment terms: net 14 days

*Statement sent
1.8*

INVOICE

14.6.0X

Mrs Jones

Partition wall   350

Payment terms: net 14 days

*Statement sent
10.7*

*rang 1.8, 'cheque in post
tommorow'*

figure 13.1 Hardip Singh's invoices

cash control and record-keeping is to file these stapled to a sheet of A4 paper, then write on the same sheet a cash reconciliation of what was in the till, split into the different types of notes and coins, then the cheques, then the credit card receipts. You will, of course, have to deduct any float that you started with. Confirm that the reconciliation adds up to the same as the till record, or calculate any 'unders' or 'overs'. If the discrepancies are small, and vary both under and over, you should have no problem with the Inland Revenue; if they are consistently under and significant you probably will.

If you do not have a till, you must have a system you stick to which ensures, again, that you do not take money out – for either personal or business use – until you have recorded that it is there. Ben Martin uses a cash bag, and makes a point of not taking out any cash until he totals up his takings at the end of the day. After totalling the takings he records them immediately in a cashbook which he keeps in the bag. He then takes out his drawings, as explained in Chapter 4, and puts the rest of the cash to one side in a separate carrier bag, ready to be banked first thing the following morning. He is careful to make sure that the takings in the carrier bag from the previous day do not get mixed up with the new takings when he starts work the following day.

Summary

- Use a system of numbered invoices – from a duplicate book, preprinted or by computer.
- Check them regularly and chase when overdue.
- Never take cash from the till without leaving a note of how much and for what; and ideally just don't take cash from the till at all.

14

receipts—paying-in book

In this chapter you will learn:
- how to fill in your paying-in book
- how to file your paying-in slips
- how to fill in paying-in books for cash- and credit-based businesses.

The aim when filling in the paying-in book is once again to link the supporting information in the file (Chapter 13) with the bank statements and the cashbook (Chapter 15), in sufficient detail that if any one of them were to be lost it would be possible to recreate the records from the others.

The point made in Chapter 3 is repeated here – do not use loose credit slips to bank your business income. Always use the slips in your paying-in book, so that there is no chance of losing them. If by any chance it is necessary in an exceptional case to break this rule, make sure that the loose slip is stapled into the latest paying-in book as soon as possible.

The suggestions in Chapter 7 about how to keep your cheque stubs apply equally to your paying-in slips – keep them together with an elastic band, and – ideally – use a box file to keep them with your other records for the year.

There is a significant difference in how the paying-in book is filled in, depending on whether it is a credit or a cash business.

Credit business

The aim is to link the paying-in slip back to the invoices, so that it is clear to anyone checking them that the payments for all the invoices have gone into the bank account.

Example

Look back at the receipts of Hardip Singh in the example in Chapter 4, Figure 4.3. He made two deposits during the month: on 10 June he paid in one cheque for £396.75, and on 20 June he paid in three cheques totalling £2750. Figure 14.1 shows both the front and back of each of the counterfoils to the paying-in slips concerned, numbers 6000132 and 6000133.

The most important point for Mr Singh to remember is that he must record the invoice numbers. This in turn means that in practice the paying-in slip should be filled in before he goes to the bank, since otherwise he does not have the information to hand. If he forgets to do this, he should at least fill in the separate amounts from the cheques on the back of the counterfoil, so that he can fill in the invoice numbers when he gets back. The other information would be easily available from the bank statement or the cashbook but picking up the invoice numbers is a lot more difficult – particularly when several cheques are submitted on the same paying-in slip.

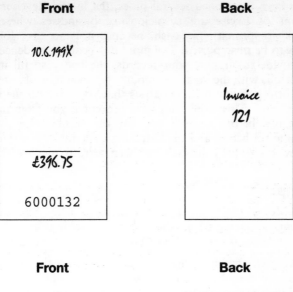

figure 14.1 Hardip Singh's paying-in slips

Cash business

For a cash business, the important thing is to match up the counterfoil to the record of takings. This should not be a problem if takings are banked daily; if more than one day's takings are banked at the same time it is a good idea to prepare a reconciliation on the face of the last takings sheet, and refer to it from the previous ones.

As has been mentioned several times, the Inland Revenue and Customs & Excise are suspicious of businesses where the receipts are primarily in cash, because it is so easy for the takings to be misreported. The more independent evidence you can provide to support your records, the better so fill in the counterfoils with the separate amounts for each type of note and coin, corresponding to the analysis that you have on the daily takings sheet. This would not have prevented you from taking money out before cashing up, but the combination of an electronic till listing and the matching cash analyses would be good evidence that your cash had been correctly dealt with.

Example

Grace Morris cashes up the takings for 3 May. She has an electronic till listing which shows her total takings as £342.56. She staples this to a sheet of A4 to form her daily takings record.

On the sheet, shown in Figure 14.2, she records the takings in the total amount of cash for each denomination of note and coin – £100 in £20 notes because she had five of them in the till etc. She comes to a subtotal for cash, then lists the cheques and totals those. She does not take credit cards, but if she did they would have been treated in a similar way to cheques. These subtotals are then added together to get the total.

The total in the till, after taking out £20 which she keeps as a float each day, comes to £345.56, so she notes on the takings record that she is £3 over. Note that she does not take this £3 out – she still records this as takings. Equally, if she had been £3 under she would have recorded the takings for the day as £339.56. Her takings are what is in the till; the purpose of checking against the till roll is to show that she has not been consistently taking cash out without recording it. It is not unlikely that there will be occasional mistakes resulting in there being slightly more or less cash in the till than shown on the listing; the important point is that there is not a consistent and significant under-recording.

Grace Morris then transfers the analysis to the counterfoil, also shown in Figure 14.2, in detail for the cash and in summary for the cheques. She bags up the coins and the notes and takes them to the bank. If there are any discrepancies when she banks the takings (because, for example, she has miscounted) she will adjust the counterfoil, and when she gets back to the shop she will make a note on the daily takings listing of the change.

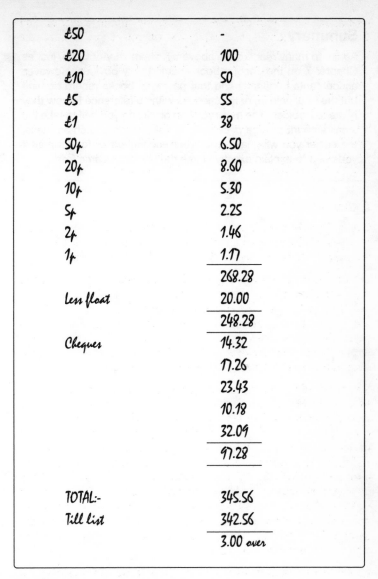

£50	-
£20	100
£10	50
£5	55
£1	38
50p	6.50
20p	8.60
10p	5.30
5p	2.25
2p	1.46
1p	1.17
	268.28
Less float	20.00
	248.28
Cheques	14.32
	17.26
	23.43
	10.18
	32.09
	97.28
TOTAL:-	345.56
Till list	342.56
	3.00 over

figure 14.2 Grace Morris' takings list

Summary

Again, to many readers the above will seem very obvious, just as Chapter 7 on the cheque book seemed very obvious. However, accountants frequently find that paying-in books record nothing but the total paid in, or list cheques with no reference to how they relate to invoices. The more you can discipline yourself to take the small amount of time necessary to keep records such as these, the easier you will make it for your accountant or for yourself if you need to explain exactly where the bankings came from.

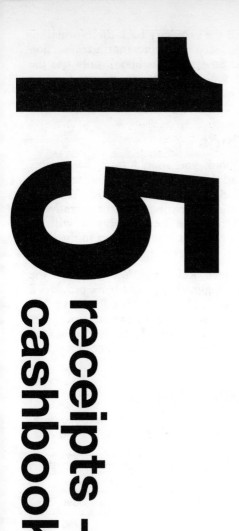

15
receipts – cashbook

In this chapter you will learn:
- how to complete the cashbook headings for receipts
- how to complete the 'narrative' column.

Having accurately recorded the necessary back-up information in the other records, the final step is to represent the transaction correctly in the cashbook. So far, the cashbook only has the payments side completed with headings; it is now time to complete the headings for receipts.

Cashbook headings

In a 32-column analysis book you should start the receipts analysis at column 22. Head this up 'Date'. Over the next three columns, 23–25, write a single heading, 'Payments in'. You treat this as one single column: it is where you record the **narrative** of what the payment is. Often the only narrative will be 'Cash/cheques', but when a payment is made direct to the bank you will need to record who it comes from.

The next column, 26, is headed 'Reference'. You enter here the reference number on the paying-in slip, if your bank provides a reference number. The next column is 'Total'. Leave the following column, 28, blank – it is used for the same purposes as the blank column on the payments side. Column 29 is headed 'Income' and column 30 is headed 'Capital introduced'.

Using the receipts columns

With the possible exception of the 'Capital introduced' column, it should be fairly obvious how the various columns are used.

Date	Payments in			Ref	Total		Income	Cap. Int.
22	23	24	25	26	27	28	29	30
10.6	Cheques			132	396.75			396.75
20.6	Cheques			133	2750.00			2750.00

figure 15.1 Hardip Singh's cashbook – receipts side

Example

Figure 15.1 shows the entries made by Mr Singh, completing the cashbook for the information provided in Chapter 4, Figure 4.3.

Notes

1 The same basic rule for filling in the analysis book applies as for payments. The total goes in the 'Total' column, and the entries in the analysis columns on each line have to add up to the same amount. In practice, until VAT is involved, the analysis is almost invariably to the 'Income' column.

2 If you want to analyse over more income columns you can do so, but this would primarily be for your own benefit. If there are two or more distinct sides to your business, and you can easily distinguish them, then it may be worth recording this extra information so that you can see which is making you the most money. Grace Morris, for example, might want to set her electronic till up to provide her with appropriate sales codes to break out the separate lines that she sells – separating newspapers and magazines from other sales. However, to make good use of this information it is necessary then to split the recording for cost of sales as well, and the time taken has to be weighed against the benefit. This sort of analysis is probably best suited to a computer.

Example

Figure 15.2 shows Ben Martin's cashbook written up for receipts in the first week of May. These are the amounts you first saw in Figure 4.5.

Date 22	Payments in 23	24	25	Ref 26	Total 27	28	Income 29	Cap. Int. 30
1.5	Balance b/f				2496.92		2496.92	
3.5	Cash				116.67		116.67	
4.5	Cash				68.56		68.56	
5.5	Cash				94.63		94.63	
6.5	Cash				72.49		72.49	
7.5	Cash				80.60	3079.87 -793.80	80.60	
	Cash contra				150.00	2286.07	150.00	

figure 15.2 Ben Martin's cashbook – receipts side

Notes

1 Because he started with a credit balance at the bank (i.e. he was not overdrawn) the balance of £2496.92 as at 1 May has to be brought in. In exactly the same way as a starting overdraft is brought in on the payments side, the starting credit balance is brought in on the receipts side. It is entered in the 'Total' column, and then included in the blank column next to it for analysis purposes.

2 You will remember that Ben Martin writes his books up as he goes, from the information on his cheque stubs, paying-in books etc. The transactions shown here only cover one week, so he is not yet ready to rule off the columns at the bottom (although if he did, and added up the totals, they would cross-total correctly). However, it is useful for him to know what the balance in his account should be. So at the end of every week he adds up the total in the 'Receipts' column (including the balance brought forward) and notes it in pencil underneath, then adds up the total in the 'Expenses' column. Subtracting the one from the other gives him the current account balance. The following week he can start from the previous subtotal written in pencil rather than adding the whole column up again.

At present the balance on the 'Payments in total' column is £3079.87 and on the 'Payments out' column is £793.80, giving a total balance in the account of £2286.07. These are, of course, the same figures as were included in the simple cashbook in Chapter 4 – the totals columns of both the payments in and payments out are the same columns as are shown in the simple cashbook. All that the analysed cashbook has done is add the relevant analysis columns.

Narrative

It may seem that the 'Narrative' column is rather useless on this side of the cashbook, since it only seems to record that cash and cheques were deposited. Here are a few examples of different narratives you may see.

Transfer from XXX If a customer pays you by a direct transfer from their account it will turn up on your bank statement with a note saying that you have received a transfer from them. Since you will not have a paying-in slip to match this against, you should also enter the invoice number here for the invoice(s) that the transfer settles.

Interest paid   If your bank account pays interest, you will get a regular credit entry for this. The analysis is taken to 'Capital introduced', because it is not treated as business income, but you must be careful to remember that it needs entering on your personal tax return.

Standing order XXX   In some businesses it is appropriate to ask customers to pay you by standing order. For payment into a business account it is not normally necessary to make any formal arrangement with your bank to do this. The correct wording of a standing order form can best be found by looking at one of the standing order forms you are asked to complete by another company, and using this as a format for your own – substituting, of course, your own bank account details for theirs!

The procedure for getting a standing order set up so that a customer pays into your account is that you first get them to complete the details on the form, including a signature and date. The form must then be returned to you. It is useful at this point to enter a reference on the form which you ask the paying bank to quote, so that you can easily identify the customer – sometimes the details that come through on your bank statement are not entirely clear. Photocopy the form for your records, then send the original to the bank branch at the address given by your customer. Payments will then come through automatically until the standing order is cancelled by the customer, or until it runs out if it was for a fixed period of time.

Summary
- Record analysed receipts in the same way as payments.
- Analyse (at least) between income and capital introduced.
- Include a credit balance at the bank brought forward.

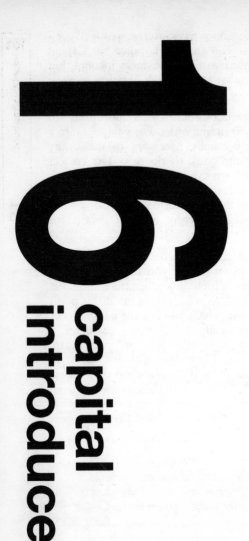

16
capital introduced

In this chapter you will learn:
- the basic principles of capital
- how to deal with more complex transactions
- which items should not be treated as capital introduced.

One of the features of this book-keeping system is that it sets out to avoid traditional accounting jargon and practices. In order to do so, it tries wherever possible not to set up what would, in other accounting systems, be credit balances on the balance sheet. It does this by treating anything which is not business income as capital introduced.

Capital introduced is the opposite of drawings. Drawings are sums taken out of the business by the proprietor; capital introduced is money which belongs to the proprietor being put into the business.

Simple introduction of capital

The most straightforward introduction of capital is when a lump sum is paid into the business account from outside. In that situation, the narrative describes where the money came from, and the analysis goes to 'Capital introduced'.

Example

Hardip Singh has sold some BT shares for £5,000, and has paid the money into the business account in order to reduce his overdraft. Figure 16.1 shows how the entry is recorded.

Date	Payments in			Ref	Total		Income	Cap. Int.
22	23	24	25	26	27	28	29	30
7.8	Cheque (BTshares)			154	5000			5000

figure 16.1 Hardip Singh – capital introduced

Notes

1 It is important for the future to have a clear explanation of where any capital introduced came from. The Inland Revenue will suspect that it comes from takings that have not been declared and have been kept in an undisclosed account or a cash hoard. When you are asked, possibly several years later, to explain the source it may well be difficult to remember. Having the source written in your accounts will be extremely useful evidence.

2 The main section in the tax return which has to be completed by the self-employed does not require you to show drawings or capital introduced. To that extent, the columns are included in the cashbook simply to allow the analysis of the 'Total' column to work. However, if you have to prepare a balance sheet, it is necessary to account for drawings and capital introduced. They will end up being netted off against each other.

More complex transactions

Two transactions which need to be accounted for using capital introduced have already been discussed – the purchase of equipment on credit and part payment of a credit card bill. If the explanation of these entries, in Chapters 10 and 11 respectively, was hard to follow, go back and look at them again now. Whilst the treatment may not be intuitive, you should remember that any funds coming into the business which are not business income are treated for the purpose of this system as capital introduced. Here are some other examples which you may come across.

Loans

Both the purchase of equipment on credit and the part payment of a credit card are examples of the same wider point – the raising of finance by means of a loan. The same treatment applies to any loan raised for the purposes of the business – the injection of funds into the business has to be recorded as capital introduced, the repayment of the amount borrowed as drawings, and the payment of the interest as an expense.

Example

The facts in Figure 16.2 are the same as in Figure 16.1, except that the £5,000 was a loan taken out by Hardip Singh to consolidate his overdraft. He is repaying the loan at £200 a month, of which £150 is capital and £50 is interest. The entries shown are for the initial payment into the current account of the £5,000 borrowed, and the first repayment.

Sometimes the repayments to a loan account will not be on a regular basis, and it will be impossible to calculate the amount of the repayment which is to be treated as interest accurately.

In that case the best approach is initially to treat all of the repayment as drawings, and to enter the interest as a contra item whenever it is charged to the loan account.

Date	Payments out	Ref	Total	Interest	Drawings
7.9	Transfer (loan rept.)		200.00	50.00	150.00

Date	Payments in	Ref	Total	Cap. Int.	
7.8	Transfer (loan)		5000.00	5000.00	

figure 16.2 Hardip Singh – loan and repayment

Example

In Figure 16.3, Mr Singh has again borrowed £5,000, but he is making repayments on an irregular basis. He makes three payments, one of £100, one of £300, and another of £250. Interest of £200 is then charged to the loan account.

Date	Payments out	Ref	Total		Interest	Drawings
7.9	Transfer (loan rept.)		100.00			100.00
7.10	Transfer (loan rept.)		300.00			300.00
7.11	Transfer (loan rept.)		250.00			250.00
30.11	Loan interest contra		200.00		200.00	

Date	Payments in	Ref	Total	Cap. Int.	
7.8	Transfer (loan)		5000.00	5000.00	
30.11	Loan interest contra		200.00	200.00	

figure 16.3 Hardip Singh – irregular loan repayment

Follow these entries through carefully. The first entry on the receipts side shows the £5,000 coming into the business current account, and being treated as capital introduced. The next three entries show the payments going out of the account, and being treated in full as drawings.

What happens next is that £200 is charged as interest, but to the loan account – not to the current account. This interest is an expense of the business, but it has not gone directly through the current account, so at present it is not recorded. In order to record it, it is necessary to use a contra item, so that the balance on the business bank account is not altered. Obviously on the payments side the amount is included in interest or in other finance charges, but what about on the receipts side?

You will remember that the opposite of drawings is capital introduced. So far all the repayments of the loan account have been treated as drawings – as if they were repayments of capital. In fact, you can now say that £200 of this total was interest. So drawings need to be reduced by £200 – and the easiest way to do that is to increase capital introduced by £200.

This is the most artificial of the capital introduced transactions, and it is made necessary because the situation really breaks one of the rules for operating this system. Right back in Chapter 1, it was stated that the system could not be used if there was more than one bank account. If a loan is being repaid on an *ad hoc* basis, the loan account effectively acts as another bank account, and the system struggles to cope with it. Any more complex system of financing than this will take the business outside the limits for this approach to book-keeping.

Equipment introduced

Fortunately this is a far easier entry to understand, even though it again involves contra entries. In some cases, the owner may put *assets* rather than cash into the business. In that case the asset needs to come into the heading of purchase of equipment, but the balance at the bank has not changed, so there must be a contra entry. Since the net result is the same as if the money to buy the asset at its current value had been put it into the business by the proprietor, and the asset then bought from a third party, it is recorded in a similar way.

Example

Figure 16.4 shows the situation after Grace Morris has been on a TV game show and won a new estate car worth £20,000 new, but only £18,000 as a delivery mileage, second-owner car. The amount to be entered for the transaction is £18,000; for tax purposes the asset must be taken at market value, and the market value at the time it is taken into the business is £18,000. This is shown on the payments side as a contra item in 'Equipment purchased', and capital allowances will be due on this as explained in Chapter 10 – even though she did not actually pay anything for it. On the receipts side the contra entry goes to 'Capital introduced'.

Date	Payments out	Ref	Total	Equipment
1.9	Contra (car won)		18,000.00	18,000.00

Date	Payments in	Ref	Total	Cap. Int.
1.9	Contra (car won)		18,000.00	18,000.00

figure 16.4 Grace Morris – equipment introduced

Items not to be treated as capital introduced

Having said that any receipt not treated as business income should be treated as capital introduced, there are some entries which can be misleading. A typical example is if a direct debit against your account 'bounces' – is not paid because you do not have enough funds. This will often be shown on the bank statement in the way set out in Figure 16.5. The debit to British Telecom for £450 appears to have gone through when it is called for by BT's bank. However, this makes the account overdrawn, and there is no authorisation for the overdraft. So the debit is not actually paid, and is credited again on the bank statement.

		Debit	Credit	Balance
3.7	DD British Telecom	450.00		-125.67
3.7	Unpaid direct debit		450.00	324.33

figure 16.5 unpaid direct debit

Rather than record this as capital introduced, the best thing to do is simply to put a line through both entries on the bank statement and not record it at all – it is a transaction which never really happened.

More difficult is the situation where the bank acknowledges that it has made a mistake in calculating interest or charges, and credits your account appropriately. If the credit is in respect of a particular charge, it may be possible to deal with it in the same way as the bounced direct debit – cross both items out on the bank statement as if they had never happened. However, when the credit is the result of a recalculation of interest over several months, for example, there may not be an exact matching entry to cross out.

The best way to deal with such an entry is as a negative payment, entering it as a *minus* figure in the payments side of the cashbook. The convention for entering minus figures is to put them in brackets, since a minus sign can easily be missed when adding up columns of figures.

Example

In Figure 16.6, Hardip Singh is recording the fact that the bank has credited his account with £100 after he queried the calculation of the overdraft interest for the previous quarter, and the bank admitted that it had charged him at the wrong interest rate.

Date	Payments Out	Total	Interest
9.10	Interest refund	(100.00)	(100.00)

figure 16.6 Hardip Singh's interest refund

Summary

Capital introduced is negative drawings.

Treat loan repayments as drawings and interest on the loan as capital introduced.

Bring assets into a business at market value with a contra to drawings.

'Bounced' direct debits etc should be dealt with by cancelling out the two matching entries where possible.

17

end of month procedures

In this chapter you will learn:
- how to reconcile your transactions with your bank account
- how to total up each month's page and check it is accurate
- how to start a new page for the next month.

Introduction

In the previous chapters you have learned how to enter the transactions which every business is likely to meet. The only ones not yet covered are VAT and wages/PAYE; these are dealt with in Chapters 18 and 19 because not all businesses will have to deal with them.

Now that you know how to record the transactions your business enters into each month, you need to know how to reconcile them with your bank account, total up the page and check it is accurate, and start a new page for the next month.

Reconciliation

The type of reconciliation you have to do depends on the way that you keep your records. For Hardip Singh, the reconciliation is part of the process of completing his books, because he doesn't write them up until his bank statement comes for the month. When it does, he sets aside a couple of hours in the evening to do his book-keeping. Starting with the payments, he enters each transaction in turn from his bank statement into the cashbook, both in the 'Total' column and the 'Analysis' column. He gets the information for the analysis from either the cheque book stub or the file of paid bills. As he does so, he puts a tick on the bottom of the stub of each cheque that has cleared through the bank. When he has entered all the payments he looks through the cheque book to find any cheques written before the end of the month which have not passed through the bank account by that time, and lists them on the bank statement.

He then adds up each column, and checks that the totals of all the analysis columns add up to the same figure as the 'Total' column. When he has confirmed that they do, he puts a small 'T' at the bottom of the 'Total' column to show that he has checked it totals both ways – down the column and along the row.

He then does the same for the receipts side of the cashbook. The final entry in the cashbook for the month is to subtract the total 'Payments out' from the total receipts, including the balance brought forward (whichever side it was on). The result should be the same as the balance on the bank statement; positive if in credit and negative if overdrawn. This is the balance which is taken forward to the next page, where the headings are written in and the balance brought forward is entered for the next month. The final version of Mr Singh's cashbook after it has been completed for June, using the entries you will now be very familiar with, is shown in Figure 17.2.

Date 22	Payments in 23	24	25	Ref 26	Total 27	28	Income 29	Cap. Int. 30
10.6	Cheques			132	396.75		396.75	
20.6	Cheques			133	2750.00		2750.00	
	Less payments out total				3146.75 T (4333.13) (1186.38)		3146.75	

figure 17.1 Hardip Singh – end of month

He has not quite finished his book-keeping. He goes through the paying-in book to see if any deposits made have not been credited on the statement. If they were paid into the account only a day or two before the end of the month they will probably appear on the next statement, so he simply lists them on the front of the statement – if the payment into the account was older than that, he may need to ring the bank and see what has happened.

He can now, finally, add the missing receipts and subtract the missing cheques from the balance on the statement. This gives him the true amount of money that he had – or that he owed the bank – at the time of the statement. This is not put into the records anywhere – it is simply a piece of information that it is useful to know.

For Ben Martin, the position is different. He has already written up his accounts as he went along, but he now needs to reconcile them to the bank statement, and undoubtedly there will be some further entries to put in. He starts with his bank statement and ticks off both on the statement and in the blank column of the cashbook used for the carry forward figure the transactions which match. If he wants to be careful, he also ticks them off against the cheque book stubs and paying-in slips. Once he has done so, he will be left with several different types of transaction.

Bank account no 123 456 23   Sort code 22-22-22   June 200X

Date	Payments out	Cheque no.	Total		Cost of sales	Employees	Admin	Motor	Travel	Advertising	Legal/ Prof	Finance	Drawings
1 Jun	Bal b/f		2,040.53	2,040.53									
3 Jun	s/o County Leasing		345.22					345.22					
8 Jun	High St Garage	234	28.34					28.34					
10 Jun	V G Browns		25.68				25.68						
12 Jun	s/o H Singh		500.00										500.00
14 Jun	Charges		42.30									42.30	
18 Jun	Anytown Courier	235	43.69							43.69			
18 Jun	Smarts	237	692.59		662.59								30.00
21 Jun	DD NICO		28.40										28.40
23 Jun	Jones Plumb.	238	254.00		254.00								
23 Jun	Post Office Counters	239	150.00					150.00					
28 Jun	Print Pronto	241	82.38				82.38						
30 Jun	DD Magnificent Mutual		100.00										100.00
30 Jun	TOTALS		4333.13	2,040.53	916.59		108.06	523.56		43.69		42.30	658.40

figure 17.2 Hardip Singh – end of month

Notes

1 Some of the early transactions on the bank statement will probably not be on the page for the current month in the cashbook. These are cheques written and deposits made in the previous month, which did not clear the bank until the current month. Because Mr Martin is recording in his cashbook at the time he makes payments and deposits, it is correct that they are recorded this way, but he needs to tick them off on the previous page of the cashbook.

2 There will be some transactions on the bank statement that do not yet show up in the cashbook, but which need to. Examples are direct debits, standing orders that Mr Martin did not remember to enter, bank charges and interest paid. These need to be entered into the cashbook now, giving the date as shown on the bank statement, even though this means that the dates on the cashbook will be out of order.

3 There will be some transactions in the cashbook which have not been ticked off (this includes those from earlier months that have not been ticked off from the current statement). These need to be written on the front of the bank statement: a list for payments and a list for receipts. By adding the receipts and subtracting the payments from the balance carried forward on the bank statement, the true amount of money at the bank or owed to it can again be calculated. This time it is a meaningful figure for the records; because Mr Martin keeps his books as he goes along, the revised balance for the bank statement should be the same as the balance to be calculated from the cashbook.

Now Mr Martin can start adding up his cashbook in the same way that Hardip Singh did: totalling the columns, checking that the column totals cross-check with the 'Total' column, and marking it with a 'T'. When he takes the total of the payments away from that of the receipts, he should get the same figure as he calculated on the bank statement.

Errors

Inevitably, the arithmetic does not always work as it should. Using a computer spreadsheet is one way of minimising arithmetic errors; this is discussed in Chapter 28.

When the problem is that the totals do not agree, the first step is to add the figures up again, to see if an error was made in keying the numbers. If there is still a problem, calculate the difference between the total you have and the total you should be getting. If there is only one error, sometimes the figure itself will give you a clue as to what it is. For example, if in Hardip Singh's case there was a difference of £42.30 on the payments side, a quick glance down the 'Total' column would show that the problem was probably to do with the charges – possibly that they had not been entered in the 'Total' column, that they had not been entered in the charges analysis column or that they had been entered in two different analysis columns.

If that does not reveal the error, see whether the difference can be divided exactly by nine. If so, there is a likelihood that a figure has been transposed when you entered it in either the 'Total' column or the analysis column; for example Mr Singh might have entered the standing order correctly to County Leasing as £345.22 in the 'Total' column, but entered £435.22 in the 'Motor expenses' analysis column. The difference is £90, which is obviously divisible by nine. If you try transposing two adjacent figures in any number you will find that the difference between the old and the new number is always exactly divisible by nine.

Finally, if none of this works, take a ruler and cross-check each individual entry with the calculator, making sure that the amounts in the analysis columns add up to the amount in the 'Total' column. Also check that the total brought forward has been entered in both the 'Total' column and the blank one next to it, and that it has been carried down to a total at the bottom of the page.

If the error is that the balance does not agree with the balance on the bank statement (as adjusted, if appropriate), again find out what the difference is. If there is only one error, the transaction can probably be identified from the amount concerned. If there is more than one error it will be necessary to look carefully and ensure that every entry on both the bank statement and the cashbook has either been ticked or properly adjusted for. If there is still a problem, it may be necessary to go through the whole ticking-off process again, this time marking a cross mark on the tick to show that the transaction has been checked again. It can be useful to do this in a different colour – red for example. It can also be helpful to use a calculator with a printout, which allows you to make sue that all the entries have been entered correctly.

Other points to note

You always start a new page when there is a new month, but you may find that you have enough transactions in the month to need more than one page. While you still have a few lines left on the first page, so as not to cramp your work, add up the totals for that page and check that they all agree. Carry all of these totals forward to the first line of the same headings on the new page, and then add up the totals again on this page to check that they agree. It is very easy here to make a copying error, and the easiest way of ensuring that you have not made one is simply to add them up again on the calculator once they have been entered.

Whether you should complete the cashbook in pencil or ink is a matter of choice. Ink gives the Inland Revenue a feeling of greater security, because it is more obvious when anything has been changed. However, in practice it is easy to make mistakes when entering transactions that are only found when you add up the columns. Continually correcting these with white fluid is messy, and it may well be better to use pencil. Much will depend on how accurate you believe you will be when you first make the entries.

Summary

- Reconcile the bank statement.
- Cross-add and reconcile the analysed cashbook.
- If there are errors, the amount of the error may indicate the problem.
- If not, and the difference is divisible exactly by 9, it may be a transposition error.

18

VAT

In this chapter you will learn:
- the basics of how VAT works
- how to record VAT as part of the book-keeping system
- when it is necessary to register for VAT.

Not all businesses will have to deal with VAT. Although VAT will be charged on many of the goods and services that a business buys, this can just be treated as part of the purchase price unless the business proprietor registers for VAT.

It is mandatory to register for VAT once your turnover in goods or services liable to the tax exceeds the registration limit in a year. The limit from April 2002 is £55,000, and it is normally increased each year at around the same time by at least the amount of inflation. Once registered, the proprietor must charge VAT on taxable supplies.

Scope of this chapter

It is not possible to give anything other than a very brief overview of how VAT works in this chapter; this book deals primarily with accounting and book-keeping rather than tax. The main purpose of this chapter is to show how VAT is recorded as part of the book-keeping system.

The first source for further information on the operation of VAT should be the local VAT office, which is under the control of Customs & Excise. On registration for VAT you should be provided with a copy of the basic VAT guide which will answer many questions relating to day-to-day problems. Up to date information about VAT can be found at Customs and Excise's website, www.hmce.gov.uk.

If you are not intending to handle your own affairs, your accountant can give you advice on VAT, and it would be a good idea to spend time discussing exactly how your business will operate, so that you are completely clear about the VAT implications of the transactions you enter into.

If you do register for VAT, be careful to read the leaflet which generally comes in the envelope containing your VAT return, as this can contain very important information – it is the method that the VAT office uses to keep in touch. In addition, there are several books available on VAT for businesses.

However, the complexities of VAT are such that you are likely to need an accountant to help you deal with it in all but the simplest of cases. Certainly someone like Grace Morris, who has a business which deals in some supplies that are liable to VAT and some that are not, would be wise at least to consult an accountant for an initial interview.

Brief overview of VAT

With that warning, the following is a brief overview of the concept and practice behind the Value Added Tax system. As its name suggests, it taxes the value that is added by a business, which it measures by comparing the taxable **inputs** to the taxable **outputs**. If a business takes in raw materials at £100 a tonne, and produces finished goods worth £300 a tonne, the value added is £200 a tonne. In practice the calculation is more complicated than that, since many other costs will have been involved in the adding of value, such as power, the use of machinery etc. All of these will be taken into account in the calculation of added value, although for VAT purposes the one major cost which is not taken into account is the cost of employees or the proprietor's time.

For a business, accounting for VAT means identifying the VAT which has been charged on all taxable supplies and goods which the business takes in, and charging VAT on all taxable supplies the business makes. Once a quarter (for most businesses), a return has to be completed and sent to the VAT office showing the tax charged on the sales made by the business, subtracting the tax included in the price paid for the supplies and goods the business bought, and enclosing a cheque (or, more rarely, a refund request) for the balance.

The term **taxable supplies** has been used several times already, and it should be stressed that the definitions of taxability have little to do with the definitions used for income tax that have been mentioned previously in this book. A supply can be **standard-rated, zero-rated** or **exempt** for VAT, depending on the exact nature of the supply concerned. This can lead to detailed analyses. For example, food in general is zero-rated. This means that a business selling food does not have to charge VAT on its sales, but may recover the VAT it pays on its business purchases – clearly an advantageous state of affairs. Newspapers and books are also zero-rated.

It may seem therefore that Grace Morris has a lot to gain from the VAT system, since her supplies are surely virtually all zero-rated? Unfortunately not. Confectionery, for example, is excluded from the general rule that food is zero-rated. Confectionery is standard-rated, which means that Grace Morris would have to increase her prices in order to keep the same profit margin on confectionery if she were VAT-registered. Items at the borderline can be very difficult to place correctly in the system – certain health food bars are sold as healthy food, for example, but are sold alongside confectionery.

The other main category – to add to the confusion – is exempt supplies. There is no need to add VAT to these supplies when they are made, but a business which only makes exempt supplies cannot recover the VAT it is charged by its suppliers in the way that a business making zero-rated supplies can. A business which makes some exempt and some zero- or standard-rated supplies is said to be 'partially exempt', and the rules for VAT recovery get very complicated indeed.

Accounting principles

There is one main concept to bear in mind when keeping records under this (or for that matter any other) book-keeping system when the business is VAT-registered. This is that the business acts as a tax collector for Customs & Excise. The VAT that it charges on the sales it makes is not really the business's money at all – it does not have to be treated as income. Instead, it is kept in a separate pot until the time comes to complete the VAT return.

Similarly, for a VAT-registered business the real cost of anything is the **VAT-exclusive price**, and this is the amount which must be recorded as an expense or cost of equipment. Again, the VAT must be thought of as something separate from the expenses, ready to be reclaimed when the quarterly accounting for VAT is carried out.

Cashbook entries – payments

It will probably not surprise you, therefore, to find that the way the VAT is recorded in your cashbook is to add a separate column in the analysis, both for payments out and receipts. Figure 18.1 shows the analysed payments for June again for Hardip Singh, but this time on the basis that he is VAT-registered. Expenses carrying VAT have now been further analysed, with the VAT-exclusive expense now appearing in the main analysis columns and the VAT appearing in a separate column at the end. Several points can be noted from this.

1 Leasing payments carry VAT; indeed a rule of thumb for deciding whether a finance agreement is a lease or hire purchase is to check whether VAT is being charged.

2 The van is used solely for business travel so there is no problem with claiming back the VAT on the fuel, provided Mr Singh remembered to ask for a proper VAT invoice. The system for cars used partly for business and partly privately is more complicated; all the VAT can initially be claimed on the fuel, but it is necessary to add a fixed amount to VAT on outputs representing the 'supply', to yourself, of some of the petrol for private use. The information needed to do this is contained in the VAT guide sent to all registered traders.

3 It can be difficult to find the amount of VAT on the small till receipts issued by shops, and for payments over £30 a proper VAT invoice should be requested. Provided you are sure that VAT is included in the price, the amount of VAT can be found by multiplying the VAT inclusive price by $^7/_{47}$. Also, a high street stationers/ bookshop is a typical example of a business selling differently VAT-rated products. Stationery is standard-rated. Books are, as mentioned above, zero-rated, so the purchase price of this book when you bought it did not include VAT. However, when you buy your analysis book it will have VAT included, because zero rating does not extend to books which are primarily intended to be filled in rather than read as they stand.

4 Bank charges are exempt from VAT, as is the road fund licence.

5 Care must be taken in dealing with the entry for the purchases from Smarts. The total purchases came to £692.59, but £30 of it was for private use – you can only claim back the VAT on business purchases. The £30 in drawings does not change, and $^7/_{47}$ of the amount previously in cost of sales moves to VAT.

6 The 'VAT' column is treated like any other in the analysis, and is totalled and brought into the check to ensure that the total on the analysis columns equals the total of the 'Totals' column. All that has happened is that each of the totals on the other analysis columns has reduced a little, to match the amount now in the 'VAT' column.

Date	Details	Total	Motor	Comms.	Drawings	Finance	Advertising	Cost of sales	VAT
3 Jun	s/o County Leasing	345.22	293.80						51.42
8 Jun	234 High St Garage	28.34	24.12						4.22
10 Jun	V G Browns	25.68	21.86						3.82
12 Jun	s/o H Singh	500.00			500.00				
14 Jun	Charges	42.30				42.30			
18 Jun	235 Anytown Courier	43.69					37.18		6.51
18 Jun	237 Smarts	692.59			30.00			563.91	98.68
21 Jun	DD NICO	28.40			28.40				
23 Jun	238 Jones Plumb.	254.00						216.17	37.83
23 Jun	239 Post Office Counters	150.00	150.00						
28 Jun	241 Print Pronto	82.38		70.11					12.27
30 Jun	DD Magnificent Mutual	100.00			100.00				
30 Jun	TOTALS	2292.60	489.78	70.11	658.40	42.30	37.18	780.08	214.75

figure 18.1 Hardip Singh – analysed payments for June, if VAT registered

Cashbook entries – receipts

Figure 18.2 shows the receipts side of Mr Singh's cashbook for June. For the purposes of this exercise it is assumed that the prices he quoted were to private customers, and that he cannot raise them simply because he is VAT-registered. As a result, $^7/_{47}$ of the receipts are now to be treated as VAT, not as his own money. Although the cost of the purchases he made has been reduced slightly by the ability to reclaim VAT, this is more than outweighed by the amount of his receipts that now goes in VAT.

This is not always the case. If your customers are mainly VAT-registered businesses, they will not be interested in whether you charge VAT or not, since they will reclaim it. It is your price before VAT that will interest them. In that situation, it can be a benefit to register for VAT even if you are under the registration limit, since you will be able to increase the price you charge to recover the VAT without it affecting your customers, but you will also now be able to recover the VAT charged on your purchases.

Date 22	Payments in 23	24	25	Ref 26	Total 27	28	Income 29	Cap Int. 30	VAT
10.6	Cheques			132	396.75		337.66		59.09
20.6	Cheques			133	2750.00		2340.43		409.57
					3146.75		2678.09		468.66

figure 18.2 Hardip Singh – analysed receipts for June if VAT registered

End of quarter

At the end of the quarter you will have to fill in your VAT return. Provided you are able to report on a cash basis, which is the normal basis for a small business, you simply add up the VAT totals for the three months. This gives you the total VAT on your outputs (sales) for the three months and the total VAT on your inputs (purchases). Take the latter from the former, and that is the VAT you have to pay to Customs & Excise.

When the cheque appears in the cashbook, it is included in the 'VAT' column for payments. As a result, if there were no further entries between the time when the quarter ended and the 'VAT' was paid over, the total in the payments 'VAT' column would now match the total in the receipts 'VAT' column. In practice, because you get a month to pay, there will normally be more entries made before then, and the normal position is that there is a permanent balance in favour of the 'Receipts' column, which increases as the end of the quarter approaches, then drops back down to a low figure when the cheque is paid out to Customs & Excise.

If you think about the nature of this balance you will realise that it is effectively a loan to you from the taxman. VAT is something that you collect on behalf of Customs & Excise, but because you only have to pay it over quarterly you get the use of the money until then. This is another advantage of VAT-registration, provided your customers are VAT-registered businesses themselves so do not mind that your prices have been increased by the tax.

Flat rate scheme

A new flat rate scheme for VAT was introduced in April 2002. It was originally opened to businesses with turnover up to £100,000, with the intention of extending it to those with a turnover of £150,000 or less shortly afterwards. Rather than the normal output tax less input tax, it offers a much simpler (if less accurate) approach. Depending on the type of business, a flat rate of VAT is applied to all the sales, without any allowance for inputs. The rate concerned depends on the main business carried on, and can range upwards from 5%. Further details can be obtained from your local VAT office.

It may well be a better scheme for many small businesses, and certainly allows them to operate VAT without necessarily needing an accountant's advice. However, if the business is unusual in the way it operates, or if it has a particularly high level of inputs, then the VAT charged may be higher than it would under the traditional system.

At the time of writing it is not entirely clear how the flat rate scheme will be dealt with on the income tax return. Expenses should now be quoted inclusive of their VAT, just as they would be for an unregistered business, but it is not clear whether the flat rate VAT is shown as an expense or is deducted from income. Check the tax return guide before completion.

Summary
- VAT is a complex tax, and all but the simplest businesses will need help.
- VAT on a gross figure can be found by multiplying by $^7/_{47}$.
- The flat rate scheme may be a better alternative for many small businesses.

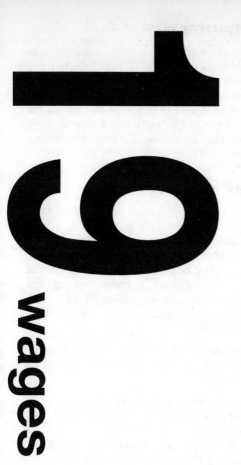

19

wages

In this chapter you will learn:
- how to deal with wages
- how to account for PAYE tax deducted and national insurance
- the business implications of employing someone for the first time.

Scope of this chapter

This chapter is concerned with the entries made in the accounting records to deal with wages, PAYE tax deducted and national insurance. As with the previous chapter on VAT, it is not possible to give a detailed explanation of how the PAYE system works, although there is a brief explanation later in the chapter, together with some consideration of the general business implications of employing someone for the first time.

Employed or self-employed?

Whether a person you take on is employed or self-employed is a crucial question for you to answer, because it drastically affects the way you need to account for the payments made to them. If you are in any doubt you should ask the Inland Revenue for guidance, and you should in any case get a copy of their leaflet IR 56, 'Employed or self-employed?'. Businesses in the construction industry should also ask for leaflet IR 148, 'Are your workers employed or self-employed?', which deals with the specific problems of that industry.

The question of whether workers are employees or not depends on the facts in each case. Some of the points that need to be considered are set out below.

- Do they work only for you, or do they work for other people as well? The more they work only for you the more likely they are to be employees.
- Do they provide their own tools? The provision of small tools may not make much difference, and is traditional in some trades, but the provision of large items of equipment is an argument in favour of self-employment.
- Are they obliged to turn up for work, and are you obliged to give them work when they do? If so, they are probably employees; if either they or you can decide that they are not working today that is a good argument that they are self-employed.
- Are they obliged to make good any mistakes in their own time and at their own expense? That is what would be expected of someone self-employed.
- Are they allowed to send someone else instead of turning up themselves? That is a very strong indication of self-employment.

- Are they paid sick pay, holiday pay etc. and do they receive any benefits in kind such as a company car or pension payments? If so, they are probably employees.

None of the above is a conclusive test although, as has been indicated, some are stronger than others. In most cases these and other factors will be looked at in the round to get a picture of the working practices concerned, and the decision will depend on that overall picture.

Consequences of employee status

Whilst this chapter is mainly concerned with the accounting implications of employee status, you should also be aware that taking someone on as an employee also brings other legal consequences. They may gain rights against being unfairly dismissed, there will certainly be 'Health and safety at work' implications, and you will probably become liable for sick pay.

However, from an accounting point of view, the main consequence is that you are again put in the position of acting as tax collector, this time for the income tax and national insurance that the employees are liable to pay on their earnings. Once you take on an employee you must tell the Inland Revenue that you are doing so, and they will send you a detailed set of instructions on how to calculate the deductions you must make and when they must be paid over.

Essentially the system is that the Inland Revenue issue a 'code number' for each employee, based on their tax position. By comparing this code number, the amount of earnings paid so far in the tax year, and the amount of tax already deducted during the year, you can calculate the amount of tax you have to deduct from this week's or month's pay. A similar (though slightly simpler) calculation will give you the amount of national insurance that has to be deducted. Only the balance is paid over to the employee.

Example

In July Mr Singh starts on a larger job, for which he needs labourers. In the past he might have taken these on as self-employed, but the Inland Revenue's advice is now that they have to be treated as employees although they are only temporary workers. He obtains code numbers for each of them, and gets the copy of the form P45 which they were given by their previous employers, which gives him the existing figures for pay and tax deducted so far during the tax year.

At the end of the first week they have both earned £300 gross. The code number and tables tell Mr Singh that he has to deduct £30 in tax from the first employee, and £25 from the second. The difference will be due to some tax allowance available to one but not the other – perhaps married couple's allowance, for example. These allowances are reflected in the code number.

National insurance (NI) has fewer complications, and both need to have £15 deducted for this. He therefore pays the first employee £255 and the second £265. They each also get a payslip showing the tax and NI deducted.

This continues for four weeks, with the same pay and tax being deducted. Mr Singh then has to account for the NI and tax deducted to the Inland Revenue. He has deducted £320 in total (4 × £35 + 4 × £45). However, as the employer he also has a liability to pay what are called **secondary** NI contributions on their wages. These come to a further £20 each a week for each employee, £160 in total. He therefore writes out a cheque for £480 to the Inland Revenue.

Figure 19.1 shows the entries made for these transactions. The payments made to the employees go into employee costs, as would be expected. The payment to the Inland Revenue also goes into employee costs, as it is partly the deductions from the wages and partly the further NI due as secondary contributions. The total of the column for the four weeks comes to £2,560, which is the £600 weekly wage bill for four weeks, plus the £20 secondary national insurance contributions each for four weeks.

Date	Payments out	Ch no	Total	Employee costs
7.7	Cash for wages	231	520.00	520.00
14.7	Cash for wages	237	520.00	520.00
21.7	Cash for wages	246	520.00	520.00
28.7	Cash for wages	252	520.00	520.00
28.7	Inland Revenue	253	480.00	480.00

figure 19.1 entries for Hardip Singh's employees

Other items that would be taken into employee costs would be pensions, staff meals etc. Even if there was no PAYE due, because the employees earned too little, the wages paid would be included in employee costs – Grace Morris includes not only the pay for the part-time worker but also the pay of the paper-boys.

Care must, however, be taken not to include either the NI contributions or tax paid for the proprietor in the 'Employee costs' column. The proprietor is not an employee, and his/her tax and national insurance are not expenses of the business – they are personal expenses. They therefore belong (as has been shown in previous examples) in drawings.

Bureaucracy of employment

Only a skeleton explanation has been given above of the bureaucracy that is involved in taking someone on as an employee. Whilst the PAYE system is very good at ensuring that exactly the right amount of tax is deducted from the employee, it is the employer who has to run the system that does this. Payslips must be prepared in an acceptable format, and end of year returns have to be made to the Inland Revenue and copies provided for the employees.

Procedures for new employees can be time-consuming, particularly if they have lost the paperwork from their previous employment. Providing that paperwork for employees leaving is equally complex and time-consuming. Whilst the system poses no difficulties for a full-time accounts and payroll department, it is not easy for a small business. There are several approaches that can be considered to minimise the disruption.

1 **Try to ensure that workers are self-employed.** They are then responsible for their own tax, and there is no need for the business owner to do anything other than pay them on invoice. However, the consequences of incorrectly categorising a worker as self-employed can be disastrous: the amount paid out can be treated as the net payment after tax deductions, and the employer has to pay the tax and national insurance calculated by grossing up this net amount. Even if it were possible to recover the tax from the employee, the rights of the employer to do so are very limited. You should therefore be very careful to treat someone as self-employed only if you are sure that they are, after consulting the Inland Revenue if necessary.

2 **Use a payroll bureau.** These are businesses who will, for a fee, handle the running of your payroll for you, producing all the necessary paperwork and letting you know how much you need to pay each employee. Their fees are generally quite competitive and reasonable, because they have a far more computerised and efficient approach than any small business could develop for itself. However, you will still need to get the details that the payroll bureau needs from the employees, and ultimately you are responsible to the Inland Revenue for the correct operation of the system.

3 **Use an employment agency.** This is an expensive option, because the agency will, of course, add its own fees. It is also not appropriate for a business which is not VAT-registered, because the employment agency charges will carry VAT. However, the great advantage is that workers can be taken on for exactly the length of time they are needed, without the paperwork problem caused in the PAYE system when workers move between employers on a regular basis.

It may be that there is no realistic alternative for a small business but to take someone on as an employee, but it would be wise to consider the options carefully before deciding to do so.

20

end of year totals

In this chapter you will learn:
- how to total your cashbook
- how to adjust for balances brought forward.

The information given in the previous chapters is all you need to know for the purposes of keeping your books on a day-to-day basis. If you are going to use an accountant to complete your figures and prepare the return, all you should do is complete the calculations shown in this chapter, then hand the book over to him or her. However, if you want to handle your own financial affairs, this chapter and the five which follow show two different methods for bringing the totals together to produce your end of year results.

The first approach is designed to produce the income and expenditure information needed to complete a tax return. For the smaller business, where the owner is happy that he or she knows the state of the business and needs little extra financial information for making business decisions, it is likely that nothing else will be required. There is no requirement for a small business such as this to produce proper accounts. The details of how to prepare this information are contained in this chapter and the three which follow.

However, some businesses may either want or need to produce a full set of financial statements, with a **profit and loss account** and **balance sheet**. These may be required by external sources, such as the bank, or a potential purchaser. They can also provide useful information to a business owner who understands them, particularly highlighting the position the business would be in if it had to pay all its creditors, sell all its assets and bring in its debts immediately. Whilst the **income and expenditure account** will give a rough and ready guide to the performance of the business over the past year, the balance sheet is a snapshot of its position at the end of the year.

Whilst some of the calculations that have been carried out in the previous chapters are also relevant for the preparation of the full financial statements, Chapter 24 starts again with the end of year totals that are explained in this chapter. It then explains a different way of dealing with them in order to produce a **trial balance**. Chapter 25 then explains how to get from the trial balance to the profit and loss account and balance sheet.

The example used in the first approach is Ben Martin, as this is typically the sort of business which does not need any more detail about its financial performance than the profit figure on which tax is due. The example for the second is Grace Morris, since when the business is eventually sold a purchaser will probably want to see the past few years' accounts. Additionally, although it does not apply to Grace Morris, such businesses are often financed by bank borrowings, and the bank would probably insist on regular sight of the accounts.

As before, it is assumed in these chapters that the year end is 31 March. If you use a different year end, you will mentally have to substitute it where you see 31 March.

Cashbook totals

When you have ruled off and totalled the figures for the month of March, you are ready to produce your final year end totals. Turn to the next page in the cashbook, and head it up as 'Year ended 31 March XXXX – summary'. Enter the usual headings at the top of the 'Payments and receipts' column which you have used to enter figures – there is no need to head up the 'Date' column, 'Payment details' column etc.

In the wide column where you normally enter the details of cheque payments, write the months of your trading year, one on each line. Then, starting with April, go back and copy the totals from each month's cashbook page into the summary, so that you end up with a line for each month summarising the total of the transactions. Remember to include the blank columns to the right of the totals on both payments and receipts, which you used in the analysis to bring forward the balance from the previous month. It is easy to make mistakes when copying the lines out, so double check that you have the right figure in the right place. As a further confirmation, you may also want to check that the totals still balance.

You then add up each of the columns again, in order to get to annual totals. In exactly the same way as the monthly totals, the analysis columns for payments should add up to the same amount as the 'Payments total' column does, and the analysis columns for the receipts should add up to the same as its 'Total' column does. If they do not add up in this way, check again that you have transferred the figures correctly, then use the same techniques as explained in Chapter 17 to see where the mistake is.

Example

Figure 20.1 shows the year end summary for Ben Martin, on the payments side of the book. Columns which he did not have to use have been omitted to save space.

Because he was always in credit with the bank, there are no entries in the blank column to the right of the total. The figure at the bottom of the 'Total' column shows that payments out in the year amounted to £17,278.56, and the analysis columns which follow show what the money was spent on. £8,952.18 was not spent on business expenses at all, it was Mr Martin's drawings.

Adjustment for balances brought forward

You will find that the figure you get in one of the totals columns is probably very high – this may be the payments or the receipts total column. The reason is that it includes the balance brought forward on your bank account every time. If you were habitually in profit, the receipts total will be high; if you were habitually overdrawn it will be the payments total. If you fluctuated between credit and overdraft, they will both be overstated.

The first thing to do is to eliminate these brought forward balances. Whatever figure you have in either (or both) of the columns totalling the brought forward balances, write it in the same column on the line underneath in brackets, and also write it underneath the 'Total' column in brackets. This indicates that you are going to subtract it, so do so, and write in the answers. Obviously when you subtract this figure from itself you will have nothing left in the 'Brought forward' column. The 'Total' column will also be reduced by the same amount. As a result, the figures will still balance – if you add up the figures in the analysis columns, now that there is nothing in the 'Brought forward' column, you will get to the new figure in the 'Total' column.

Example

The way this works can be seen in Figure 20.2, which shows the receipts side of the year end summary for Ben Martin. The 'Total' column adds up to £53,513.74, but this figure is meaningless on its own. All the brought forward bank balances of about £3,000 a month are included in it. These add up to £34,622.60. This sum has to be eliminated from the total to come back to a figure which genuinely does show the amount that has been paid into the account – £18,891.14.

Month	Total		Cost of sales	Admin	Motor	Travel/ Subs	Advertising	Drawings
April	1,297.26		143.80	23.46	350.00		140.00	640.00
May	1,202.79		213.45		430.34	34.00		525.00
June	1,138.54		123.54	12.00	350.00			653.00
July	2,177.01		134.29	45.23	654.23		54.00	1,289.26
August	1,190.89		210.89		385.00			595.00
September	1,191.53		145.29	16.24	350.00			680.00
October	1,744.41		134.93		723.94		265.54	620.00
November	1,367.26		218.82		382.23	68.21		698.00
December	1,374.81		268.23	22.58	350.00			734.00
January	2,138.32		187.20		480.00	25.20	120.00	1,325.92
February	1,321.46		162.00	76.23	541.23			542.00
March	1,134.28		134.28		350.00			650.00
Total	17,278.56		2,076.72	195.74	5,346.97	127.41	579.54	8,952.18

figure 20.1 payments year end summary, Ben Martin

	Total	Brought fwd.	Income	Cap. Int.
April	4,060.90	2,496.92	1,563.98	
May	4,312.87	2,763.64	1,349.23	200.00
June	4,239.20	2,710.08	1,529.12	
July	4,587.89	3,100.66	1,487.23	
August	3,564.00	2,410.88	1,029.12	124.00
September	4,118.26	2,373.11	1,745.15	
October	4,551.97	2,926.73	1,625.24	
November	4,304.85	2,807.56	1,497.29	
December	4,987.71	2,937.59	2,025.12	25.00
January	5,306.19	3,612.90	1,693.29	
February	4,636.12	3,167.87	1,468.25	
March	4,843.78	3,314.66	1,529.12	
Total	53,513.74	34,622.60	18,542.14	349.00
	(34,622.60)	(34,622.60)		
	18,891.14			

figure 20.2 receipts year end summary, Ben Martin

Further adjustments

If you look at the cashbook now you may feel that you already
have the information to enter into the tax return, since you now
have a total figure for virtually every box in the schedule
reporting your business income. However, there are still some
major adjustments that need to be made before the figures can
be used. These are covered in the next two chapters.

Summary

- Prepare a page with monthly totals.
- Add them up and cross-check.
- Eliminate balances brought forward.

21 adjustments for payments

General principles

The figures you were left with in Chapter 20 showed how much money you spent during the year and how much money you received. But it does not necessarily show what you really earned. Look at these simple examples of a month's trading by two different market traders selling CDs.

Mr Lennon buys 100 CDs for £5 each. He sells them all during the month for £10 each. His income and expenditure figures on a cash basis show purchases as £500 and sales as £1,000.

Mr McCartney buys 200 CDs for £5 each. He sells 100 of them during the month for £10 each. His income and expenditure figures on a cash basis show purchases as £1,000 and sales as £1,000.

Would it be correct to say that Mr Lennon made £500 profit in the month but Mr McCartney only broke even? Surely not, as Mr McCartney sold as many CDs as Mr Lennon, and made the same amount of profit on each one. The difference is that he still has some left to sell – he has some **stock**.

A similar problem can arise if bills have been received but not accounted for. For example, Mr McCartney might have received and been billed for his 200 CDs but not yet paid the bill. If he still sold 100 of them his books would show no payments out but £1,000 received. It would be wrong, however, to suggest that he had made £1,000 profit, as he has not yet paid for the goods he has sold.

Adjusting for these points is known as adjusting from a **cash basis** to an **earnings basis**. This is a useful piece of jargon to know, because in some situations the Inspector of Taxes may ask you on which basis your figures are calculated. It is strictly not acceptable any longer to prepare accounts on a cash basis, although where any adjustments would be minor the Inspector may sometimes accept it.

Cost of sales

The adjustment for cost of sales in a business that sells goods is an adjustment for stock. If you have stocks of materials or goods in your business, it is essential that you carry out some form of stock-take on the last day of trading. The aim is to find out how much stock you have on hand at the end of the year, and to value it at the amount it cost you, or the amount you could receive for it in the normal course of trade, whichever is the lower. In practice this means valuing at the amount you paid for it unless it could now only be sold at a loss.

As evidence, you should have a written list of the stock on hand at the end of trading at 31 March, plus its value at cost.

A manufacturing industry will have three different types of stock – **raw materials, work in progress** and **finished goods**. These all need to be valued at cost or value, whichever is lower. For raw materials the principles are straightforward, but when you value work in progress and finished goods at cost you must make an allowance not just for the raw materials that have gone into them, but also for the wages, heat light etc. that have been used to make them. One approach is to decide how many weeks' production is tied up in the stocks and take an appropriate proportion of those costs for the year. Above all, to satisfy the Inland Revenue, you must be consistent in the way that you value stock.

Service industries do not have stock as such, but they may have carried out work which has not yet been billed. This is accounted for as work in progress, but since they are unlikely to have a cost of sales figure, the adjustment is normally made to income – this is covered in Chapter 22.

Other adjustments

The other figures are generally easier to find. At the end of the year, on the last day of trading, write 'unpaid at year end' on each invoice in your filing system that has still to be paid (i.e. is still above the divider card). You can then, when you come to write up the books, list the unpaid bills and total up the amounts for each category of expenditure. Remember to include only the VAT-exclusive figure if you are VAT-registered, since you will offset the VAT against your input tax. If you are not VAT-registered, you include the full amount.

Recording the adjustments

You should now have the stock sheet, with the value of stock and work in progress and totals for the unpaid bills. These need to be entered in the payments side of the year end summary, a couple of lines below the totals and any adjustments made as detailed in the last chapter. In the details column write 'Stock at end of year' and write the total figure for stock into the 'Cost of sales' column. Put brackets round it, as it is to be deducted.

If this is the first year of trading you will simply have to deduct the figure for stock from the cost of sales purchased during the year to get the true cost of sales figure. But if this is not your first set of accounts you must add on the stock from last year. Last year you will have excluded it from that year's cost of sales because it was still unsold. This year you have probably sold it, and if not it is reflected in the stock figure for this year. So you must now add on the stock figure from last year. Look the figure up, on the next line of the summary write 'Stock at beginning of the year' and write it in under cost of sales. Complete the sum to get your true cost of sales for the year.

A similar process is needed for the unpaid bills. On the next line, write 'Creditors at year end' (your creditors are the people who give you credit) and fill in the totals under the appropriate headings. These are going to be added to the payments totals, because they are expenses you still have to pay which relate to the current year. On the next line, unless this is your first set of accounts, write 'Creditors at start of year' and fill in the figures from the previous year end, in brackets as they are to be deducted. Again, complete the sums and you have the true expenses on an earnings basis.

Finally you must make sure that you do not lose the sheets you prepared, giving you the details of these adjustments. It is a good idea to staple them into the cashbook on the page after the annual summary. Alternatively, if you have a box file for the year in which you are keeping your cheque stubs etc., the sheets can go in there.

Example

Ben Martin does not have stock as such, so there is no stock adjustment in his accounts. You will see an adjustment for stock in subsequent chapters when Grace Morris prepares her figures.

However, Mr Martin's cost of sales figure shows his payment for fuel. Virtually all of this is the bill he pays for his fuel card at the beginning of each month, but this is paying off the cost of fuel purchased and billed the previous month. This is therefore an unpaid bill which he must account for. As at the year end he had a bill for £155.26. The bill for £143.80 paid in the first

	Total	Cost of sales	Admin	Motor	Travel/ Subs	Advertising	Drawings
Total	17,278.56	2,076.72	195.74	5,346.97	127.41	579.54	8,952.18
Creditors at y/e		155.26		68.00			
Creditors at start		(143.80)					
TOTAL		2,088.18		5,414.97			

figure 21.1 adjustments for payments, Ben Martin

month of the year related to the previous year. So in Figure 21.1 he has adjusted for these. He also has a bill outstanding at the year end for £68 for some repairs to the taxi, so this is included as a creditor. He had no other creditors at the start of the year. So his cost of sales figure is now £2,088.18 and his motor expenses £5414.97. There are no other changes to his payment figures.

Possible adjustments

In theory, many other adjustments could be made to Mr Martin's accounts. Some of the advertising bills he paid later in the year may relate to advertisements that still have some time to run – should he adjust his figures to reflect this? He will receive a telephone bill in a month's time, some of which will relate to the previous two months – should he adjust for this?

In practice, for a small business, it is unlikely that the Inspector of Taxes will be bothered to have you make minor adjustments such as this. However, you must not exploit the system. You must be consistent in the way that you treat expenses year on year, and you must not deliberately try to get bills delayed so that they come in after your year end.

Summary

Make adjustments for:
- Stock
- Creditors
- Any other major payments in advance.

22

adjustments to receipts

In this chapter you will learn:
- how to adjust your receipts
- how to calculate your debtors at the year end
- how to calculate your work in progress.

In the same way as the payments needed adjusting in the last chapter, the receipts may also need adjusting for matters that relate to the year in question, but which are not yet in the cashbook.

There are potentially two main ways that the income figure may have to be altered. The most obvious is that work may have been billed but not yet been paid for.

Debtors

In order to calculate this, on the last day of trading, write 'unpaid at year end' on all invoices issued but not yet paid on 31 March. When you are ready to write up your books, you can list these invoices out on a separate sheet of paper and add them up. These are your debtors at the year end. Enter them on the year end summary in a similar way to the adjustment for creditors in the last chapter. You need to add the debtors at the end of this year, but subtract the debtors at the end of the previous year.

At the same time, you may need to consider the problem of bad debts. Most businesses that sell on credit eventually suffer some bad debts, where it proves impossible to recover the money billed. At the year end, you may have some bills such as this where you have given up all hope of recovering the money. Provided you are either not registered for VAT or are trading on the cash basis, you can simply draw a line through the invoice and ignore it, not including it in your debtors at all, nor in the doubtful debt provision described below. Since it has not yet been included in your cashbook at all, you treat a bad debt as if it had never arisen in the first place.

However, if you think you may not get paid but are not really sure, you can make a **provision for doubtful debts**. Typically you would do this if there was some dispute over the bill or you were chasing for payment without success. Estimate the likelihood that you will not, in fact, get paid, multiply the bill by this percentage, and treat this amount as your doubtful debt reserve. For example, if you are owed £1,000 and you think there is a 75% chance that you will not get paid, you will have a doubtful debt reserve of £750.

The Inland Revenue will only allow a deduction for doubtful debts if they are 'specific', i.e. related to a particular bill. You cannot say that, on average, you find 10% of your debts go bad and you are therefore going to make a 10% provision; you have to say that you expect a particular debt to go bad for a specific reason and make a provision against it.

For the time being note the amount you have calculated as your doubtful debt provision at the end of the year, on the sheet where you listed the debtors. It is a good idea to give as much information as you can on the sheet, explaining why you made the doubtful debt provision, in case it should later be challenged. You do not need to make any cashbook entries for the doubtful debt provision – it will be entered when the figures are transferred to the tax return. Include all doubtful debts in full in your adjustment for debtors; it is only bad debts (ones you have already completely given up on) that you exclude.

Work in progress

The other adjustment that you may need to make, as was mentioned in the previous chapter, is for work in progress in a primarily service-based industry. The problem here is typically that clients are billed only when work is complete, and at the year end some of the work is not. However, some of the costs of the work have been incurred, and it is therefore correct that the work in progress should be valued at cost and added to the sales for the year.

From a practical point of view, if the business you are in consists of providing your own skills and labour, and does not involve you in direct costs for particular jobs nor in employing staff, the adjustment you would have to make for unfinished work in progress is so small that it will not be necessary to do so. The reason is that the proprietor's own time and effort is not a cost to the business, and work in progress has to be valued at cost.

However, if the work, or some of it, is actually completed and has simply not yet been billed, then you will have to include it. If you are in any doubt about the need to make an entry, ask for advice from the Inland Revenue.

The entry is made in the way that will by now be familiar to you: add the work in progress at the end of the current year to receipts, and subtract the work in progress at the end of the previous year.

Example

Ben Martin does not issue invoices, but he does have a debtor at the end of the year. The work that he did for Cab-U-Like during March will not be paid to him until April. This amounts to £142. Similarly, the work he did in March the previous year was paid to him in April this year. He included this amount, £126, in the previous year's accounts, so needs to exclude it from this year's. He therefore adds £142 and subtracts £126 from the income figure – see Figure 22.1.

	Total		Income	Cap. Int.
Total	18,891.14		18,542.14	349.00
Debtors at y/e			142.00	
Debtors at start			(126.00)	
TOTAL			18,558.14	

figure 22.1 adjustment to receipts, Ben Martin

23

transfer to tax return

In this chapter you will learn:
- the format of the self-assessment tax return
- how to complete your tax return.

Format of self-assessment tax return

Tax returns for the year ended 5 April 1997 and later years come under the self-assessment system. So far as the self-employed are concerned, this means that instead of submitting their accounts and a tax computation in order to settle their tax liability, a schedule in the form has to be completed. The tax return form including this schedule is only sent to the self-employed; employees receive a return with pages that relate to employment income instead.

It should be stressed that unless the business owner wants to, there is no need to complete proper accounts: it is only necessary to complete the boxes as requested. If accounts (more properly called **financial statements**) are prepared, then the balance sheet details can also be entered on the tax return form, but for a smaller business there is no requirement to do so.

Indeed, for businesses with a turnover of less than £15,000 a year, the return of business income can be reduced to a three line entry – income, total expenses, and the difference between the two as a profit or loss. However, even if the business does fall within these provisions, it is still wise to keep records in the format used throughout this book. It allows you to complete the more detailed schedule if your turnover should prove to be more than £15,000, and it provides you with some worthwhile detail about the different types of expense you incur.

This chapter does not explain in detail how to complete the tax return; that is beyond the scope of the book. What it does is explain where the figures as calculated for business income and expenditure need to be entered. Up to date information about income tax can be found at the Inland Revenue's website, www.ir.gov.uk.

Details of the income and expenditure schedule

The tax return has a section headed 'Income and expenses' in the self employment pages. This has a box numbered 3.16 for the business income, then two parallel columns of boxes for the expense headings. The column on the right-hand side is where you enter the figures calculated in the last chapters. The column on the left-hand side is for disallowable expenses; whilst most of these never get entered into this book-keeping system, you will see below that Mr Martin has to adjust for private use of his cab.

Example

Figure 23.1 shows the boxes as completed by Ben Martin; the design of the return will vary slightly from year to year but it is likely that you will be able to identify these boxes clearly. Most of the figures can be traced back quite easily to the year end summary as amended, but there are some changes.

1 Mr Martin keeps a record of the mileometer reading when he starts work and when he stops. From this he can calculate that 5% of his total mileage is private. He therefore calculates 5% of the fuel costs in cost of sales and 5% of the motor costs and includes these figures in the disallowable boxes alongside.

2 Although he does not use his home very much for business purposes, it is still where he garages the cab and works on it. He is therefore entitled to include part of his home expenses as a deductible item in the accounts. Rather than go into a complicated calculation, Mr Martin estimates a cost of £5 a week and includes this in the figure for premises costs.

3 Mr Martin pays his son £3 a week pocket money provided he cleans the cab at weekends. Allowing for holidays, he includes £141 in employee costs for this.

The rest of the entries are straightforward, and can be completed by following the guidance in the helpsheets issued by the Inland Revenue. The boxes for capital allowances also need to be completed on the following page, using the figures calculated in Chapter 10.

Finally Mr Martin uses the large box for additional information to explain that he has estimated his use of home expenses as £5 a week, that he has calculated his private mileage from a log kept daily, and that no other disallowable expenses were included in his accounting records. There is no set format or requirement to include information here, but it is useful to explain anything that you think the Inspector might query.

TRADING AND PROFESSIONAL INCOME
for the year ended 5 April 200X

Income (turnover)

6.16 £ *18 558*

- Cost of sales   6.17 £ *104*   6.13 £ *2088*

- Construction industry subcontractor costs   6.18 £   6.34 £

- other direct costs   6.19 £   6.35 £

Gross profit/(loss) 6.36 £ *16 470*

other income/profits 6.37 £

- Employee costs   6.20 £   6.38 £ *141*

- Premises costs   6.21 £   6.39 £ *260*

- Repairs   6.22 £   6.40 £

- General administrative expenses   6.23 £   6.41 £ *195*

- Motor expenses   6.24 £ *270*   6.42 £ *5414*

- Travel and subsistence   6.25 £   6.43 £ *127*

- Advertising, promotion and entertainment   6.26 £   6.44 £ *579*

- Legal and professional costs   6.27 £   6.45 £

- Bad debts   6.28 £   6.46 £

- Interests   6.29 £   6.47 £

- Other finance charges   6.30 £   6.48 £

- Depreciation and loss/ (profit) on sale   6.31 £   6.49 £

- Other expenses   6.32 £   6.50 £

Total expenses 6.51 £ *6716*

Net profit/(loss) 6.52 £ *9754*

figure 23.1 Ben Martin's tax return

24

trial balance

In this chapter you will learn:
- how to put together a basic set of accounts in a standard format
- what the jargon really means.

Introduction

As explained in Chapter 20, this chapter and Chapter 25 deal with 'proper' accounting, and allow you to put together a set of accounts in the standard 'profit and loss account plus balance sheet' format. Whilst the method explained here should allow you to produce such a set of accounts, and should in particular prevent you from ending up with a set of accounts that don't balance, it is obviously not possible to teach much more than the basic mechanics of producing accounts in such a short space. It also takes some short cuts, particularly in the calculation of some items on the balance sheet, where the correct method of calculation would simply take too long.

It is strongly suggested that you avoid trying to put together a set of accounts such as this unless you absolutely have to. In practice, the figures entered into your tax return (including those for capital allowances) as explained in the previous chapters, together with a brief statement of the debtors, creditors, stock and bank balance, should be enough for most small businesses. However, if you want to do so, read these chapters carefully.

Jargon

So far we have avoided jargon. It is not possible to do so any more. To begin with, you have to understand the difference between the profit and loss account and the balance sheet.

The profit and loss account is essentially the information you entered in the income and expenses columns of your tax return. It shows the performance of the business over the whole year. The balance sheet is like a snapshot at the end of the year. It shows the assets you have, and who they belong to, on the last day of the trading year.

A balance sheet is called a balance sheet because it balances! It shows all the assets you own – equipment, stock, debtors, cash – *less* the money you owe (creditors). It then shows who that belongs to, which will be you or the partners in the business. It does this by always ensuring that there are two entries for everything – a **debit** entry and a **credit** entry.

So far, the system in this book has managed to achieve the same without referring to debits and credits. Remember, everything in the bank book has been entered twice, once in the 'Total' column and once in the analysis columns. You now need to learn what those entries are in accounting terms.

On the payments side of the book, the entries in the 'Total' column are *credit* entries to your bank account, and the entries in the analysis columns are *debit* entries to expense accounts, drawings or asset accounts.

On the receipts side, the entries in the 'Total' column are *debit* entries to your bank account, and the entries in the analysis columns are *credit* entries, either to income accounts or to capital introduced (i.e. the opposite of drawings).

If you are VAT-registered, the entries on the payments side are *debit* entries showing VAT reclaimable from Customs & Excise; the entries on the receipts side are *credit* entries showing VAT payable to Customs & Excise.

This is the point at which many people decide that they either do not need a proper set of accounts, or that they are going to have a qualified accountant prepare one for them! If you still want to continue, note that the bank account entries will seem to be the wrong way round. On your bank statement you will be used to seeing payments out as debits and payments in as credits. This is because the bank statement shows your accounts in the books of the *bank*, not in your own books.

Trial balance

It should be evident at this point that when you get to the stage of calculating the end of year totals, i.e. after making all the adjustments shown in Chapter 20, the total debits and credits balance. The 'Total payments out' is a credit, which is matched by the 'Total debits' in the analysis columns of payments out. The 'Total payments in' is a debit, which is matched by the total of the analysis columns for payments in which are all credits. The trick is to keep that balance. This means that you have to obey one fundamental rule:

> **For every debit there must be an equal and opposite credit – and *vice versa*.**

As you see how this chapter and the next unfold, you should keep this in mind.

To draw up the trial balance, you need to convert the figures you produced in Chapter 20 into a vertical format. Start on a new page of your cashbook, and write headings down the wide column on the left-hand side. The first heading should be 'Bank', the others should reflect the headings from your cashbook. You only need one VAT heading.

Then label the first two cash columns 'Cashbook', and the first one 'Dr' for Debit and the second 'Cr' for Credit. Start by entering the total payments out in the 'Cr' column and the total receipts in the 'Dr' column, both against the heading 'Bank'. Then enter each of the analysis totals for payments out into the 'Dr' column opposite the appropriate heading, and the payments in analysis totals against their headings in the 'Cr' column. The only two headings which should have an entry in both Dr and Cr are those headed 'Bank' and 'VAT' (if you are VAT-registered). Total the columns and check they still balance.

Next, unless this is your first year of trading, head the next two columns 'Opening balances' and label them 'Dr' and 'Cr' again. This is where you have to enter the balances from the previous year's balance sheet. If you don't have a balance sheet from the previous year, but this is not your first year of trading, you would need to draw one up – that is beyond the scope of this book and is almost certainly a job for a qualified accountant.

Looking carefully at the balance sheet, it should be quite easy to see which balances are debits and which credits, and how they balance when set off against each other. The debit balances are all your assets – equipment (after deducting depreciation), stock, debtors and cash. These are most of the entries at the top of the balance sheet. The main credit balance will normally be right at the bottom of the balance sheet: it is the figure of profit retained in the business, normally shown as the result of a brief calculation – profit brought forward, *plus* profit for the year, *less* drawings. The only other credit balances you are likely to find are those for creditors, which will have been deducted somewhere in the top half of the balance sheet as part of a calculation of 'current assets', a bank overdraft and possibly a longer-term bank loan which may be shown in the bottom half of the balance sheet.

You will have to write new headings for all these items except for 'Equipment' and 'Bank' – add these to the left-hand column, then enter the debit and credit balances in the 'Opening balance' columns. Add up the two columns and check they still match.

You have now entered the opening balances and cash book movements for the year. Chapter 25 will show you how to make the other adjustments. To end this chapter, Figure 24.1 is the trial balance of Grace Morris showing these entries using simplified figures to make it easier to follow. In Chapter 25 we shall see how to get from there to the final accounts.

	Cashbook		Opening balance	
	Dr	Cr	Dr	Cr
Bank	93,000	85,500	6,000	
Cost of sales (purchases)	50,000			
Employee costs	4,000			
Premises costs	5,000			
Administrative	1,000			
Motor	1,000			
Advertising	500			
Finance charges	1,500			
Equipment	2,500		4,000	
Drawings	15,000			
Income (sales)		85,000		
Capital introduced		1,000		
VAT	5,000	7,000		
Stock			3,000	
Debtors			500	
Cash			100	
Creditors				1,000
Profit retained				12,600
Depreciation				
Profit for year				
	178,500	178,500	13,600	13,600

figure 24.1 opening balances and cashbook movements

Summary

- Don't prepare a proper set of accounts unless you have to.
- Enter the opening balances onto the trial balance.
- Trial balances must balance!
- For every debit there must be an equal and opposite credit.

25

final accounts

In this chapter you will learn:

- how to adjust payments
- how to complete your final accounts.

Adjusting payments

You should at this point look back at Chapters 21 and 22. The adjustments that you are about to make are the same as those that are described there, and although the mechanics of making the adjustment are explained here, the way you arrive at the figures is not repeated.

Label the next two cash columns as 'Payments' and then mark them 'Dr' and 'Cr' respectively. The first thing you want to do is the equivalent of 'adding back' the opening stock and the opening creditors to purchases.

It is essential, below, that the only creditors are for purchases. If there are other creditors you will have to adjust the other expense headings accordingly.

Make a 'Cr' entry for stock to match the 'Dr' opening balance. Now make a matching 'Dr' entry against purchases. Then make a 'Dr' entry to match the creditors' opening balance and make a 'Cr' entry against purchases.

In the 'Dr' column enter the closing balance for stock, and in the 'Cr' column the closing balance for creditors. Make matching, but opposing, entries against purchases. You have to write neatly to fit both figures in! If you are unclear about what these entries achieve, look back at Chapter 21 and you will see that they are the same as the calculations carried out there, except that here we now have a record of the stock and the debtors, whereas before they were incorporated into the cost of sales figure.

Add the two columns up, and check that they balance.

A similar exercise now has to be carried out for receipts. Label the next two cash columns 'Receipts' and enter 'Dr' and 'Cr' respectively. Enter the opening balance for debtors against the heading in the 'Cr' column, with a corresponding amount in the 'Dr' column against sales. Enter the closing balance for debtors against the same heading but in the 'Dr 'column, and enter the same amount in the 'Cr' column against sales. Total the two columns just to prove that the entries match and the columns balance.

Figure 25.1 shows Grace Morris's entries for the 'Debtors' and 'Creditors' columns – the other headings are omitted for simplicity. She has the following to adjust for:

- Creditors £2,000 at end, £1,000 at start.
- Debtors (for newspaper delivery) £800 at end, £500 at start.
- Stock £3,500 at end, £3,000 at start.
- Depreciation £1,300.
- Cash on hand £50 at end, £100 at start.

Other adjustments

Head the next two cash columns 'Other adjustments'. The extent to which you need these depends on how sophisticated you want your accounts to be. As explained in Chapters 21 and 22 there are many matters which can be reflected in the accounts if you want to do so, trying accurately to match the income and expenditure, but the only one that you are almost invariably going to come across is **depreciation**.

Depreciation has been ignored so far, because it is not taken into account for tax purposes – capital allowances are given instead. The idea of depreciation is that you should write off as an expense each year a proportion of the cost of your plant and equipment, so that it reduces to its disposal value at the end of its useful life. In practice you will be best using a set formula such as 20% a year.

Enter a new heading in the left-hand column – this is an expense heading, like general administrative expenses or motor expenses – called 'Depreciation expense'. Enter in the 'Dr' column of 'Other adjustments' the depreciation charge for the year, and in the 'Cr' column enter the same amount against the heading for equipment. On most sets of accounts you will actually find the original cost of the equipment and the figure for accumulated depreciation kept separately, but that gets more complex, and offers little information that is of use to you.

If the amount of cash on hand has changed, take the difference to income. See Figure 25.1.

	Payments		Receipts		Other Adj	
	Dr	Cr	Dr	Cr	Dr	Cr
Bank						
Cost of sales (purchases)	2,000 3,000	3,500 1,000				
Employee costs						
Premises costs						
Administrative						
Motor						
Advertising						
Finance charges						
Equipment						1,300
Drawings						
Income (sales)			500	800		50
Capital introduced						
VAT						
Stock	3,500	3,000				
Debtors			800	500		
Cash				50		
Creditors	1,000	2,000				
Profit retained						
Depreciation					1,300	
Profit for year						
	9,500	9,500	1,300	1,300	1,350	1,350

figure 25.1 payments, receipts and adjustments

Final accounts

Label the next two columns 'Profit and loss account' and the following two 'Balance sheet' with 'Dr' and 'Cr' columns as before. You are now going to total across for each heading, and enter the final figure in the appropriate column for Profit and loss or Balance sheet. The easiest way to do this is to calculate the profit and loss figures first, because these are all the headings that appeared in your original cashbook headings *excluding* bank, VAT, drawings, capital introduced and equipment purchased, but *including* depreciation expense if you have provided for this. All the other headings go to the balance sheet.

In order to add up the rows, you should look first to see whether, overall, the credits or the debits for the line are higher. With most entries this should be easy – expenses are always going to end up as debit totals, income as credits, assets as debits etc. For totals which are going to end up as debits, add up all the debits on the line, deduct the credits and enter the balance in the 'Dr' column of either the 'Profit and loss' or 'Balance sheet' sections. With totals that are going to end up as credits it is the other way round – add up the credits, deduct the debits, and put the answer in the 'Cr' column. You will find that the figures for closing stock, debtors and creditors will all be as you expect; what may be more surprising is that the bank balance should also be correct. If you look at the entries this is not so surprising – you have taken into account the starting balance, the total of payments in and the total of payments out, so naturally the result is the closing balance.

The final calculation is to add a further heading to the left hand column, 'Profit for year'. Add up the total of the 'Cr' column for Profit and loss, then subtract all the entries in the 'Dr' column. Enter the balance that is left in the 'Dr' column of Profit and loss and the 'Cr' column of the Balance sheet section. You should then find that all the columns balance. If when you are doing this calculation you find that the total of the 'Dr' column exceeds that of the 'Cr' column then you have made a loss, and the figure goes in the 'Cr' column of the Profit and loss account and the 'Dr' column of the Balance sheet.

This is hard to understand without trying it, so at this point you may like to go back through this chapter and Chapter 24, writing up the trial balance for Grace Morris and then extending it to prepare the Profit and loss and Balance sheet columns. Include £1,300 for depreciation expense. Compare your answer with Figure 25.2.

	Profit & Loss		Balance Sheet	
	Dr	Cr	Dr	Cr
Bank			13,500	
Cost of sales (purchases)	50,500			
Employee costs	4,000			
Premises costs	5,000			
Administrative	1,000			
Motor	1,000			
Advertising	500			
Finance charges	1,500			
Equipment			5,200	
Drawings			15,000	
Income (sales)		85,350		
Capital introduced				1,000
VAT				2,000
Stock			3,500	
Debtors			800	
Cash			150	
Creditors				2,000
Profit retained				12,600
Depreciation	1,300			
Profit for year	20,550			20,550
	85,350	85,350	38,150	38,150

figure 25.2 trial balance

Finally you need to enter these figures from the trial balance columns onto a set of accounts. This is just a matter of laying the figures out in an accepted format. Follow the example in Figure 25.3 for Grace Morris. Note that if she was overdrawn at the bank, the bank figure would be a credit in the Balance sheet columns of the trial balance, and would appear with Creditors in the balance sheet itself.

Summary

It is likely that you have concluded by now that preparing proper accounts such as this is too difficult. The advice given at the beginning of Chapter 24 is repeated – don't bother to prepare them unless you absolutely have to. If you do want to, and you need further information about drawing up final accounts, you should get a copy of *Teach Yourself Basic Accounting*. Although this teaches a traditional double-entry system of book-keeping, once you have prepared the initial trial balance as set out in Chapter 24, the principles which it explains for drawing up accounts can still be applied.

Balance Sheet

Fixed assets:

Equipment		5,200

Current assets:

Stock	3,500	
Debtors	800	
Bank	13,500	
Cash	150	
		17,950

Current liablilities:

Creditors	2,000	
VAT	2,000	(4,000)
		19,150

Represented by:

Profit retained	12,600	
Profit for year	20,550	
Capital Introduced	1,000	
	34,150	
Less drawings	(15,000)	
		19,150

figure 25.3a final accounts for Grace Morris

Profit and loss account

Sales		85,350
Less: Cost of Sales		(50,500)
Gross Profit		34,850
Less:		
Employee costs	4,000	
Premises costs	5,000	
Administrative	1,000	
Motor	1,000	
Advertising	500	
Finance charges	1,500	
Depreciation	1,300	
		(14,300)
Net profit for the year		20,550

figure 25.3b final accounts for Grace Morris

26

budgeting and cash-flow forecasting

In this chapter you will learn:
- how to budget for the future
- how to plan your expenditure
- how to keep your finances in check.

Most of the accounting we have looked at is backward-looking – telling you how well you have performed. But to keep proper control of your business you also need to be forward-looking, planning how much you are likely to spend and keeping your finances in check.

Every book on running your own business will advise you to budget and forecast your cash-flow. It has to be admitted that the majority of small businesses don't bother. However, if you can get into the habit of doing it, it will pay dividends. As always, the intention in this chapter is to give you an approach for doing this that will minimise the amount of work involved.

The way in which budgets and particularly cash-flow forecasts are laid out is called a **spreadsheet**. If you are familiar with computers, you will know that a spreadsheet is a common type of computer program. Two of the most well known are **Lotus 1-2-3™** and **Microsoft Excel™**, although both are major programs with a lot of features that you will not need. There are also many other programs that are similar in principle but are far cheaper (and work on far less powerful computers) because they only include the basic features.

Spreadsheet programs are, as you might expect, ideal for setting out this sort of information, particularly because they allow you to change your assumptions and see the effects flow through the spreadsheet. There is more advice on this in Chapter 28, on computerisation.

Budgeting

Budgeting is an essential part of **costing**, which is dealt with in the next chapter. A large part of budgeting is the sort of calculation that you will be familiar with from your own personal finances. You will be used to calculating how much your monthly outgoings are, anticipating quarterly bills such as the telephone, and so on. All these skills can also be used in budgeting for your business.

However, there is an important distinction in budgeting between fixed and variable costs. Take Grace Morris' shop as an example. Some of her costs are fixed. That includes not just the amounts that she can predict in advance, such as the business rates; it also (in her case) will include her electricity bill, for example. Unless she changes the hours that she opens, her electricity bill is unlikely to be much affected by the amount that she sells. Whether the shop gets one customer an hour or twenty, she will use roughly the same amount of electricity.

However, other costs will vary directly with the sales. The most obvious is cost of sales – clearly if sales double, cost of sales will probably double as well. For Grace Morris that is likely to be the main variable cost. Although she may have to go to the Cash and Carry more often, it is unlikely to make that much of a difference or be that directly related to sales.

For Hardip Singh it is likely that far more of his costs will vary directly with sales. Materials clearly will, but cost of labour is likely to do the same, as is hire of machinery.

Layout of a budget

The distinction between variable and fixed costs becomes obvious when the layout of the expenses is considered. Figure 26.1 shows Hardip Singh's budget for the three months ending in October. Whilst it is common and probably better to be budgeting monthly, it is obviously preferable to have a quarterly budget than none at all. Hardip Singh finds it easiest to have a three-monthly budget based on his VAT quarters – as he has to have his accounts prepared for the VAT return it does not take much longer to fill in the actual outcome of the three months on his budget sheet.

The first heading is 'Sales'. This figure is the sales invoiced during the period, not necessarily the cash received. For Hardip Singh this is simply found by quickly totalling the invoices in his book that are outstanding at the end of the three months, adding this to the figure entered on the VAT return for income received, and subtracting the invoices that were outstanding at the end of the last quarter. It is necessary to compare sales invoiced because the other direct costs are likely to reflect the work actually done during the quarter, not the work which has been paid for.

Looking first at the headings, 'Materials', 'Labour' and 'Other' direct expenses (meaning hire of machinery in this case) are the first expense headings under sales. These are totalled and deducted from sales to give a figure known as **gross profit**.

It is going to be difficult to predict what the gross profit will actually be. What should not change too much, however, is the

	Budget	Outcome	Variance	Reason
Sales	25,000	22,000	−3,000	
Direct expenses				
Materials	6,000	6,000	−	
Labour	6,000	5,500	−500	
Other direct	500	500	−	
Gross Profit	12,500 (50%)	10,000 (45%)	−2,500 -5%	Paid for materials and labour R. Henderson, not billed
Other expenses				
Motor	500	490	-10	
Admin	1,500	1,700	+ 200	Stationery
Advertising	500	510	+10	
Net Profit	10,000	7,300	−2,700	

figure 26.1 three-monthly budget Oct–Dec, Hardip Singh

gross profit ratio – the percentage you get when you divide the gross profit by the sales and multiply by 100. If the direct expenses are genuinely moving in line with the sales, the ratio will stay the same. It is for this reason that the Inland Revenue look closely at variations in gross profit ratios, inevitably assuming that the reason for a variation is that income is being understated.

After this come the other, fixed, expenses. These should be fairly predictable, and the main concern will be whether they have been correctly forecast. This is therefore a good time to look at the figures entered.

In the first column of figures Hardip Singh enters his **budget** for the period. He estimates that he will have sales of £25,000, and that in all the direct expenses will take 50% of that. After that he has various self-evident fixed expenses, giving him the expected profit of £10,000 for the quarter.

The second column shows the **outcome**. Sales are lower than expected, and the gross profit percentage is also lower. Most of the fixed expenses are more or less in line with what would be expected, but general administrative expenses are higher.

There is, of course, no point in preparing the figures if you do not analyse them. The best way to do this is shown in the next two columns. The first of these shows the difference between the budget and the outcome. In the next column, Mr Singh has set out the reason for the difference.

There is no explanation for the reduction in sales – he was simply not as successful as he had hoped. That, however, does not explain why the gross profit ratio is lower. Looking at his records Mr Singh can see why: he has already paid for some materials and labour for a job that has not been finished and therefore not billed. There is also an explanation for the extra general administrative costs: he has had new stationery printed for which he had forgotten to budget.

The only part of this that gives cause for concern is that sales are lower than expected. Mr Singh needs to look at ways of getting more business, or alternatively accept that he is going to have a lower profit than he expected.

Cash-flow forecasting

You can't start cash-flow forecasting until you have some idea of budgeting, but cash-flow forecasting adds the additional element of estimating the cash needs or resources of the business over the coming months. Cash-flow forecasting really does need to be done monthly if it is going to be useful, and is an essential tool for predicting problems with your overdraft limit before they arise.

Essentially, cash-flow forecasting is an exercise in predicting what your cashbook totals are going to look like. In doing so, you must remember that the date you invoice is not necessarily the date you receive the cash, and so on.

Example

Hardip Singh is going to see his bank manager because he wants to take on a major job for the next four months. He will be paid on a **cost plus** basis, that is to say he will be paid his costs in full plus a profit margin which covers his own time and his profit.

In this particular case the 'plus' is a 20% markup on his costs. However, the costs will be substantial: £8,000 a month, of which £3,000 will be materials and £5,000 labour. He can delay paying the materials bill until a month after it is received, but he will have to pay for labour each week. He will be paid for materials two months in arrears, but the rest of the payment will not come until two months after the work is completed.

Figure 26.2 is a cash-flow forecast just for this particular job – in practice you normally do a forecast covering all the headings in your cashbook for the whole of your business, but this example is simpler to understand. In the first month the only entries are expenses – £5,000 for labour, since he will not have paid the first materials bill yet. This means that by the end of month 1 his overdraft will increase by £5,000 to fund the work. In month 2 he still receives nothing, but pays out £8,000 to cover £5,000 for labour and the first bill for materials, so his overdraft has gone up by a total of £13,000 by the end of month 2. In months 3 and 4 he receives £3,000, refunding his materials costs from months 1 and 2, but pays out for materials bought in months 2 and 3. He also pays his workforce as before, so by the end of month 4 his overdraft is up by £23,000 in total. Month 5 is in balance – the work is finished so he does not have to pay labour; he pays the materials bill for month 4 but he gets the reimbursement for his materials in month 3. Finally in month 6 he gets the payment covering month 4's materials, the £20,000 he has paid in labour and the 20% profit, which leaves him with the expected cash surplus.

This is, of course, a forecast – things may turn out differently. However, on the basis of this information Mr Singh can go to his bank manager and ask for an increase in his overdraft limit of £23,000 for six months. In practice he would try to build in some leeway – say £30,000 for seven months in order to cover any additional costs and late payment.

Month	1	2	3	4	5	6
Income	–	–	3,000	3,000	3,000	29,400
Outgoings:						
Materials	–	(3,000)	(3,000)	(3,000)	–	–
Labour	(5,000)	(5,000)	(5,000)	(5,000)	–	–
Balance b/f	–	(5,000)	(13,000)	(18,000)	(23,000)	(23,000)
Balance c/f	(5,000)	(13,000)	(18,000)	(23,000)	(23,000)	6,400

figure 26.2 cash-flow forecast, Hardip Singh

Summary

- Budgets allow you to compare your expected results with the actual results.
- Budgets use sales and purchases, not cash received and paid.
- Cash-flow forecasting uses estimates of the cash coming in and going out.
- Cash-flow forecasting is based on budgets, but with adjustments for timing differences.

27

costing and pricing

In this chapter you will learn:
- how to price your goods or services
- the dangers of underpricing
- how to remain competitive while still making money.

Introduction

Costing is a subject in itself, and there are many different systems for allocating costs to production. In a small business, however, these are generally unnecessary, and it is certainly unlikely that owners of small businesses will have time to implement a proper costing system. Some indications of the factors that business owners can think about are set out below, but nothing more.

The main area in which costing is investigated in this chapter is the aspect of pricing. There is a tendency for small businesses to under-price, trying to compete solely by being cheaper. Research suggests that this is likely to lead to business failure, and that a proper understanding of how to price, based on costs, will help a business survive.

Costing

One of the elements which many business owners may forget to include is the cost of their own time. If you run a business you expect to get something out of it. Your work is probably the most valuable that your business can offer – you must ensure that the cost of your time is reflected in your calculation of the costs of the output.

In a service industry, the time spent by staff in general is likely to be the most important element of costs. Ensure that it is properly recorded, by means of a time sheet.

Remember the cost of keeping stock can be high. Buying stock in bulk can be tempting, but it can increase your overdraft, cause storage problems, and result in unsaleable stock that has to be scrapped or at least reduced below cost to sell.

Pricing

In order to understand how to price items, you need to return to the concept of fixed and variable costs, referred to in Chapter 26. You can see that if an item is sold for more than its variable cost, you will make a **gross profit**. So for Grace Morris, broadly, if she sells an item for more than she paid for it she makes a gross profit. However, if she sold everything for one penny more than she paid for it, she would soon go out of business – she would make a gross profit but she would not cover her overheads, and therefore would not make a **net profit**.

In order to set her prices, Grace Morris needs to start by establishing an overall mark-up that she wants to achieve. To begin with, she needs to estimate the cost to her of the stock that she thinks she will sell in a week. Say this is £2,000. Next she needs to estimate her total overhead costs for the year, and divide that by 52 to get a weekly figure. That might come to £200. Finally she needs to add on the cost of her own time – say £300 a week. So every £2,000 of stock she buys has to sell for at least £2,500 in order to cover her overheads and profit; she needs to mark up her goods by at least 25% on average.

So far, so good, but that is not the end of the story. What if Grace Morris is approached by a local camp site, say, which runs a small site shop? In the past they have bought their own goods from the Cash and Carry, but it is proving time-consuming. Is she prepared to sell £500 of goods a week to them at a discount of 10% from her normal prices?

It would be wrong for Grace to think that she cannot reduce her prices in this way. This is additional business, over and above the business she is already getting. She will supply goods for £450 that would normally sell at £500 in her shop. However, the goods will only have cost her £400. Her overheads will not alter, so she will make an extra £50 profit each week.

Good pricing is all about balancing the need to make enough sales at a sufficient mark-up to cover your overheads, together with exploiting the opportunity to make genuinely additional sales at anything over their marginal cost.

Sometimes in practice there is little discretion over prices – there is a market rate and you have to meet it. The calculation can then be carried out the other way round. Say, for example, Grace Morris knows that she is only going to be able to achieve a markup of 20%, because she needs to compete with other shops. She still has to make an extra £500 a week to cover her overheads and the cost of her own time. If this is to be only 20% of the cost of the goods she sells, it follows that she must sell £2,500 of goods a week in order to do so. If she does not, it will eat into her profit – the reward for her time. Alternatively she can look at changing the mix of goods she sells in order to achieve a higher gross profit, or cutting her overheads.

Normally business owners need to use both approaches flexibly. It is not possible simply to set your own prices without reference to those of competitors, but on the other hand if you simply compete on price you will need to turn over a substantial volume in order to make a profit after overheads. Pricing is sometimes more of an art than a science, but a sound understanding of the principles outlined above will help you to make adjustments based on more than just guesswork.

28

computerisation

In this chapter you will learn:
- the principles of spreadsheets
- how to choose an accounting package
- how to back up your system.

Introduction

You do not need a powerful computer in order to get rid of some of the drudgery of preparing accounting records. Using the information in the rest of this book, you can set out your records on a spreadsheet instead of a handwritten cashbook, and the spreadsheet will handle the calculations for you. Alternatively, and preferably with a fairly up-to-date computer, you can use one of the accounting packages that are on sale.

Spreadsheets

The cashbook is nothing more than a series of spreadsheets, and there is nothing to stop you setting one up using *any* spreadsheet program. The computations involved are simple, and as a result the simpler the spreadsheet program the better. If you have a high-end office suite such as **Lotus Smartsuite™** or **Microsoft Office™**, and you are not familiar with the spreadsheet package, you will probably find that you can set up a table in the word processor program which will do the job just as well and will be less daunting to use. On the other hand, if you can get to grips with the spreadsheet package, you will probably be able to get much better analysis data from it, including pie charts and bar graphs showing patterns of income and expenditure etc.

The best approach is to draw up a standard format spreadsheet including all the headings, which you save and then load under a different name for each month. Remember to set the options in the spreadsheet for **currency** format (two fixed decimal places) and for **brackets** to show negatives.

A useful way of checking that the rows of analysis have been correctly entered is to put a check formula at the end of the row, which adds up the analysis entries and subtracts it from the total. It is then easy to check quickly that these all equal zero: if one does not there is an error in the entry that needs correcting. A similar technique can be used to cross-check the totals at the bottom of the sheet.

Depending on how good the package is, it may be possible to load all the months of the year on separate sheets of a '3D' spreadsheet, and then 'drill down' to get the totals calculated in Chapter 20 automatically.

Accounting packages

It is strongly recommended that you do not spend money on the more complex accounting packages for a small business. Indeed, the programs sold primarily as personal finance organisers such as **Quicken™** and **Microsoft Money™** are normally good enough to handle small business accounts prepared on a bank account basis as described in this book. Some transactions may not always be easy to enter, but with the understanding you will have gained from this book you should be able to come up with a way of entering most transactions that ensures they are accurately recorded. If you are going to use a basic package such as this, however, make sure that it will handle VAT if you are (or are likely to become) VAT-registered.

Back-ups

The one advantage of a manual method of keeping a cashbook is that it is far harder to lose. Electronic information is far too easy to delete by accident. Keep a separate back-up copy of everything you do on computer, and ensure you update it on a regular basis. Also print out your records so that you have a paper copy.

Stationery list

This appendix sets out a 'shopping list' of stationery for you to buy, indicating when you are likely to need it. It covers only the stationery you will need for preparing and filing your accounting records, not the other business stationery such as letterheads and compliment slips that you may require.

You can find these in large stationery shops, or at business stationery suppliers. Initially it is probably best to go to a shop where you can look at what you are buying to check it is what you need; once you are used to the system you will probably find it is cheaper to buy future supplies from a discount mail-order stationer.

- **32 cash column analysis book**. This is described and illustrated in Chapter 8. An alternative is a loose-leaf book, but it is then easy to lose a sheet when you take the sheets out after the year ends.
- **Lever arch file for invoices paid**. This should be a large file, with rings about 5 cm high. The lever arch mechanism and clip to hold the papers flat is important; you will be continually opening and closing this file, and it needs to stand up to the heavy use. Don't be tempted to buy a four-ring file unless you have a four-ring hole punch!
- **Divider card**. To separate the paid and unpaid invoices.
- **Either: Another lever arch file and divider card, or a duplicate invoice book**. These are sold pre-numbered with carbon sheets. You will want to start a new one each year, so don't get a 250-sheet book if you are going to issue only 50 invoices. Make sure you buy the invoices version, not statements or orders.

- **Bulldog clip**. If you bought the duplicate invoice book above, to show where the first unpaid invoice is.
- **A4 paper**. You'll probably have this anyway, but you need it to fasten till receipts etc. to.
- **Box file**. Get one with a retaining clip to hold the papers down and a catch to hold the lid in place when it is closed. This is going to hold your cheque book stubs, paying-in book counterfoils, invoices paid and invoices received, when the year is finished; it needs to hold them all securely.
- **Calculator**. If you don't already have one you will need a calculator to add up your figures. You do not need a complicated scientific or financial calculator, but a memory and (if VAT registered) a percentage button are useful. The most important thing is that it should have large enough buttons and a clear enough display for you not to make mistakes. If you find you have a lot of trouble getting your totals to tally, it may be useful to buy a calculator with a print-out, so that you can easily check that you have entered all the figures. However, these are normally desk-top machines, and are more expensive.
- **Stapler**. Large, office size, so you can staple all the receipts to the back of your petty cash listings.
- **Treasury tags**. These are the pieces of green string with metal tags on the end that you can use to hold together hole-punched papers. Get the long ones, so that you can fasten together your invoices, bank statements etc. at the end of each year before putting them into the box file.
- **Petty cash box**. Not essential – you can use a biscuit tin – but it does make it easier to count the money and keep the receipts.
- **Petty cash slips**. Again not essential, but they are cheap and will remind you to fill in things like the date.

appendix 2

Sales of assets in a full set of accounts

Undoubtedly one of the most difficult things to deal with in preparing a full set of accounts is the sale of a fixed asset such as a car or a piece of machinery. There are basically three ways of approaching it.

Method 1

You can simply treat it as a negative expense, as set out on pages 63–4. This will give you a set of accounts that balance, but the statement of your fixed assets on the balance sheet will not be in the normal accountancy format, not will it give the same figure that a conventional set of accounts would give.

Method 2

You can keep a strictly correct set of records showing acquisition costs and accumulated depreciation. Essentially this involves not deducting the depreciation from the cost of the assets each year, but keeping a running total of it, and showing in the balance sheet the assets at their original cost, then subtracting the accumulated depreciation over the years. When the asset is sold you deduct the original cost from the assets. The total depreciation charged on it from accumulated depreciation and any profit or loss is shown as a separate item in the expenses on the profit and loss account (as a negative if it is a profit). The resultant balance sheet figures for fixed assets, accumulated depreciation and the net difference will be required by traditional accounting. If you are going to follow this approach you really need to get a book on traditional accounting, such as *Teach Yourself Basic Accounting*.

Method 3

This is the method to use if you feel you need a set of accounts that gives the same figure on your balance sheet as traditional accounting, although with a slightly unorthodox layout. It will work only if you rarely sell equipment, because there is quite a lot of work involved. It gets to the same net result as method 2, by a similar calculation, but without keeping accumulated depreciation records. You should make these adjustments to your trial balance before you make the calculation for depreciation this year, and it is assumed that you have already recorded the sale proceeds as negative expense, as explained on pages 63–4.

1 Find the original cost of the assets you sold.
2 By looking at the percentage you used to calculate depreciation in preparing your final accounts (see p. 134), calculate the total depreciation you have deducted so far from this asset. Remember that each year you are applying the percentage to the reduced balance – e.g. if a computer cost £1,000 and you depreciate by 20% a year, in the first year you deducted £200, but in the second year you deducted only £160 (£1,000 – £200 × 20%).
3 Subtract the depreciation from the cost. The figure you get is called the 'net book value' – the amount that is in your balance sheet at the moment for this asset.
4 Look at how much you recorded as a negative expense for the money you received when selling this asset. Was this more or less than the net book value? If it was more, you made a profit on sale; if it was less you made a loss. Calculate how much the loss or profit on sale is.
5 If you made a profit on sale, the entries are to credit the depreciation expense account and debit the plant and machinery account with the profit. If you made a loss, the entries are to debit the depreciation expense account and credit the plant and machinery account with the loss.

You can then calculate the depreciation on the remaining balance in your plant and machinery account as before and prepare the final accounts. You should change 'Depreciation' in the profit and loss account to 'Depreciation and profit/loss on sale'.

Depreciation is meant, over the years, to reduce the value of the asset to what it will be worth when you sell it because it no longer has any use to you. If you make a profit on the sale, that means that too much depreciation has been charged overall; if you make a loss, it means too little has been charged. These entries therefore simply reverse those 'mistakes'.

index

setting up a small business
vera hughes & david weller

- Are you setting up a small business?
- Do you need help to define your product or service?
- Are you looking for guidance in marketing and finance?

Setting up a Small Business helps you with all the everyday aspects of running a small business and gives detailed guidance on specialised areas such as legal requirements, opening a retail or office-based business, staff selection and marketing.

Vera Hughes and **David Weller** started their own business in 1980, having been involved in the retail industry for many years. They have written a number of books on retailing.